WOODST★R
CAFÉ
NORTHAMPTON, MA

MEETING
STREET
CAFÉ
PROVIDENCE, RI

Cafe
Solterra
JEKYLL ISLAND CLUB HOTEL, GA

LEVAIN
BAKERY
MANHATTAN, NY

UMQUAT
MAE
ATHENS, GA

SATCHEL'S
PIZZA
GAINESVILLE, FL

FIT
and
FUEL
CAFE
NAPLES, FL

ASK A
PRO

ASK A PRO

DEEP THOUGHTS AND UNRELIABLE ADVICE FROM AMERICA'S FOREMOST CYCLING SAGE

PHIL GAIMON

VELO
PRESS®

BOULDER, COLORADO

3002 Sterling Circle, Suite 100, Boulder, Colorado 80301-2338 USA

VeloPress is the leading publisher of books on endurance sports. Focused on cycling, triathlon, running, swimming, and nutrition/diet, VeloPress books help athletes achieve their goals of going faster and farther. Preview books and contact us at velopress.com.

Distributed in the United States and Canada by Ingram Publisher Services

A Cataloging-in-Publication record for this book is available from the Library of Congress.
ISBN 978-1-937715-72-4

This paper meets the requirements of ANSI/NISO Z39.48-1992 (Permanence of Paper).

Illustrations by Daniel Seex
Interior design by Vicki Hopewell
Interior photographs courtesy of Phil Gaimon, except: Lyne Lamoureux, p. 9; Stefano Barberi, p. 26; Danny Munson, p. 59; iStock, pp. 66–67; Michelle Blake, p. 123; Frank Overton, p. 155.
Composition by Jessica Xavier

Text set in Fuse V.2

17 18 19 / 10 9 8 7 6 5 4 3 2 1

DEDICATION

I've always made an effort to save everything I write, but when it was time to collect my old columns for this book, I realized that "Ask a Pro" had survived four laptops and three e-mail platforms over the years, and I had many months missing. Desperate and afraid, I handled this problem the way I've handled so many problems over the years: I called my mom. She'd saved every issue of *VeloNews* since I started and happily scanned the months I was missing.

CONTENTS

INTRODUCTION

Cycling is a puzzling sport, filled with rigid etiquette, creepy clothing, complicated equipment, and annoying rules. It's intimidating for beginners and downright impenetrable if you want to compete. How full do you pump your tires? What do you eat before a ride? Bib shorts or regular shorts?

For better or worse, I was a quick study, and once I took up cycling I figured out the basics quickly. When I turned professional with Jelly Belly at 23, my friends thought I had it made. I showed up for the group ride with a jersey covered in candy, my name on my helmet, and a bike I got for free. I let everyone notice how awesome I was, and then I dropped them. My salary was only $2,000 that year, but I had them so fooled that doctors and lawyers asked for training advice, and racers begged to know how they could join me in the pro peloton. Quickly tired of answering the same questions over and over, I pitched an idea for a Q&A column to *VeloNews* magazine, and "Ask a Pro" was born.

At first I sort of played a character in my monthly column: the know-it-all cocky pro. He was ironic and fun, because I knew nothing back then, and he was a loser by almost any standard. As the column progressed, and as I actually became a decent bike racer, I found that I had more stories to tell, and so the character faded out. Then I joined the WorldTour, and while I still don't know it all, I do know most of it when it comes to this silly sport.

Reading all of those columns straight through in preparation for this book was kind of like watching myself grow up. I rolled my eyes at the sophomoric humor that made me laugh when I was 24 and noticed that the column got more sincere and introspective when I began writing my first book, *Pro Cycling on $10 a Day*. Reflecting on my past as I worked on the manuscript gave me a sincere desire to share what I'd learned, to prevent people from making the mistakes I had made—unless I thought of a good sophomoric joke instead.

As I progressed from a young professional on a small team to a seasoned WorldTour rider, writing was my creative outlet between races, and I reliably sent in my "Ask a Pro" column every month. But now, after eight years of racing full-time, I'm moving on from pro cycling (partly because pro cycling has moved on from me). I could probably keep the column going and continue answering your questions, but even though I've only been an amateur for a few weeks I can already feel that I'm losing my credibility. And as a retiree, I'm quickly becoming a grumpy old man.

Besides, in the last couple of years, when I asked readers what they wanted answered in the next issue, I'd get 5 questions about urine, 10 about farts, 60 about poop, and a handful of general bad jokes (I tell the bad jokes, thank you very much). I suppose a handful of bad jokes is better than a handful of poop (like I said, I tell the bad jokes), but I've answered all the questions by now, sometimes more than once, and I can't do it anymore. It's time for you people to leave me alone.

I'm grumpy, but I'm still a softie. I wish I'd had someone to answer my dumb questions over the years, and I did like being the question-answerer in the magazine. I also have a warm feeling about *VeloNews* for being the first suckers to offer me a regular writing gig, which became a big part of my life. So while I have stopped the column cold turkey, I've also put together this complete collection of your questions and my answers. In these pages, you can find everything you need to know about cycling from a pro cyclist, in a form you can easily read while you poop. I'm telling you everything here, for one last time, with some bonus content. I've also added some footnotes, in part because some of the columns needed an update and mostly because my past self deserves to be called out and teased.

PART 1
NEO PRO

In January 2011, I turned 25. Racing for Kenda Pro Cycling on a salary of $15,000 per year, I'd been dominating the local amateur races, but my best results as a professional were unimpressive: a stage win at the 2009 San Dimas Stage Race and second overall at the 2010 Tour of Taiwan. I started writing the column after I'd moved to Baltimore, Maryland, in a misguided effort for a climber to escape Florida's criterium scene after college.

Q I've got an old Bottecchia with a classic Team ADR paint scheme that I used to race on. I commute on a Specialized Tri Cross, and I want to have a second bike in the garage for training. Do you think it's worth trying to update it, or am I better off just selling it and getting something more modern? It seems like upgrades could be difficult because of the older Campy stuff it's equipped with, but I've got a sentimental attachment to this heavy cro-mo bike from college.

It sounds like you've got things mixed up a bit, with a fancy bike for commuting and a beat-up old one for training. Use the Bottecchia for commuting, maybe setting it up as a fixie.* It's a cool old bike, and you don't need a high-performing, smooth-shifting, fancy machine to get around town. Sell the 'cross bike and get a new road bike to train on instead.

If you can afford it, though, the best bet would be to just buy more bikes and keep them all. I don't see how anyone can get by with less than seven bikes. Remember Maslow's hierarchy

---

* Proof that I was into fixies before the hipsters.

of needs from college psychology class? Me neither, but it went something like food, shelter, sex, commuter bike, track bike, 'cross bike, mountain bike, race bike, time trial bike, and backup race bike. You're not even halfway there yet, and who are you to argue with the founder of modern psychology?

Q **I'm 17 and a new racer. I've started shaving my legs, and my girlfriend makes fun of me for it. How can I be accepted by my friends?**

I remember the first time I shaved my legs. It was hard to explain in high school, and the truth behind leg shaving is that there's really no good reason for it, other than being accepted by the racing community and looking cool. Would you rather look cool to bike racers like me or to losers at school? That's what I thought.

As far as the girlfriend, she'll get used to it, because you have nice legs and she gets to admire them. Soon she'll be reminding you when it's time to shave. That's when you break out the altitude tent and start doing other masculine bike-racer things, like counting calories and eating salad. Either way, though, you're 17, so you should break up with her.

Q **Why do so many pro riders still feel the need to train with no helmet? Do they feel that their riding is so good that a traumatic head injury could never happen to them? Or is there a more complex reason?**

That's a darn good question. A lot of guys are too cool for helmets, which makes them just cool enough for debilitating brain injuries. Why don't they wear them? The wind in your hair is a pleasant feeling. If the benefit of a nice breeze outweighs the perceived risk of crashing, a confident rider might leave the helmet at home.

The biggest factor for pros is probably social. At a group ride in Australia or Europe (even today),* you're the weirdo who sticks out if you wear a helmet, because most people don't. Every year, though, you hear of some big name who spent time in the hospital because a cat ran into his wheel on a training ride. As a somewhat frequent crasher, I wear my helmet everywhere—sometimes even at the dinner table or in the bathroom. You never know when a cat could come out of nowhere and take you out.

Try not to be the helmet cop, though. Right or wrong, no one likes to be told what to do. If someone shows up on

---

* This was years-ago-today. Helmets are more the norm today-today.

your group ride sans helmet and crashes, you're not legally obligated to peel their brains off the pavement, and you can take their wallet if nobody's looking.

Q I've been suffering from saddle sores. Do you use chamois cream? How much should I use?

Chamois cream exists for a reason. It lubricates the area to reduce chafing, and some of the fancier ones kill bacteria. I use Chamois Butt'r because they sponsor my team and the company has always been nice to me, but in my experience all the brands work pretty well.

Avoid some of the old-school cheap solutions, like Bag Balm and plain Vaseline. They'll stop the symptoms and you'll save a few bucks, but your saddle will get all slimy and disgusting, and you'll quickly find yourself tired of explaining it when someone touches your bike and then recoils in horror.* Your nether regions are important. Spend the money.

Also, be careful with quantity. Don't spread it all over your shorts like it's Country Crock. Put the shorts on, then reach in and apply directly to the sensitive areas of your skin. In

---

* This part was mostly directed at my teammate, David Guttenplan, who might still be a Bag Balm user. Don't touch his saddle.

most states, it's a good idea to avoid eye contact with anyone nearby while your hand is in your pants.

Q What kind of power numbers do you put out at threshold? I want to see how I stack up.

Waaaaay more than you do. You should quit.

Q Can you get me on your team or give me your director's information? I met you that one time, I placed third in the crit last week even though I had a flat tire, and I beat you in a town-line sprint on a group ride two years ago.

Okay, no one sent me that question verbatim, but I get variations of it from dozens of riders every year. Don't get me wrong: I remember when I was the young guy trying to break into the pros, but I've begun to dread these interactions. For one thing, I'm worried about my own contract 10 months out of the year, so I can't stress about yours. The real truth, though, is that no one can get you on a team but yourself. The contract comes when you have results at some bigger races and you've shown that you're good enough to contribute to a pro team. If you're good enough, you don't need my help to get on a team, and if you're not good enough, I wouldn't help you anyway.

For contact info, USA Cycling's website has a club listing by state, with contact info for every club manager, including professional teams (which are designated by "UCI" on the page). I could send you all the contact info you need, but you should go through the website and find them all yourself, because that's how I did it, and then it won't be my fault that Frankie Andreu's BlackBerry keeps blowing up.

Also, for the record, I let you beat me in that sprint.

Q **You've said you're a clean rider. How do you face the sport with the constant stream of riders getting caught and suspended for doping? Can you really compete clean?**

In the U.S., I'm sure it's not that much of a problem, because I know I'm clean and I consider myself about as competitive as everyone else. I do hope to race at the top level someday, and I fear things are worse in Europe, although they seem to be improving. Am I undertaking an impossible quest? Time will tell. If bike racing doesn't work out, I'll push boulders up hills and then watch them roll back down.

Q **Dear Sir or Madam, I work in the foreign Payment Department of WEMA BANK PLC LAGOS NIGERIA. There is an account opened in our bank in 1990 but since 1996**

My CLEAN tattoo, before it was touched up by a better tattooist. If you get a tattoo, spend as much money on it as you can.

nobody has operated on this account again. After a private investigation I discovered that the owner of this account was the manager of U.MARTINESCO.LTD—a foreigner who has since died without having a beneficially to this account. The amount contained in this account is US$19,780,000. My colleague and I will need you to set up a new account for this transfer and send to us. Or you might send an existing account with no fund in it for us to use. For your help, you will get 20% of the recovered funds.

Contact me urgently for more details.

—*Best Regards, Mr. George Eze*

Well, readers, it looks like I've hit the big time. This sort of opportunity is one of the perks of being a professional athlete. I'm off to the Aston Martin dealership. Until next month.

Have a question for me?

E-mail it to phil@philthethrill.net. The best question each month will receive a free jersey from SharetheDamn-Road.com.*

Q In women's cycling, the use of the term "pro" can be ambiguous. What is the proper definition of a pro?

The term definitely has a broad range. Some riders feel "pro" because their bar tape matches their kit and they bought a name sticker to put on their bike's top tube. For men, you're technically a pro when you're on the roster of a UCI-registered professional team, although your salary might make you feel like an intern. Personally, even though I have "pro" on my license, I'll still feel like I'm living a lie until my monthly check buys more than an airport burrito on the way to the race.

---

* This was the clothing business I'd started back then. I made it into a few stores, started getting clubs to do big orders, and did well enough that team clothing sponsors got understandably mad because I was competing against them. You can still buy a Share the Damn Road jersey, but it's been a long time since I had anything to do with it. I don't know if we ever gave away the free ones I promised here. Sorry.

You're right that it's more ambiguous for women, since fewer teams pay the UCI fees—or salaries at all. If you subjected them to the same qualifications I had for men, there'd be awfully slim fields, but there are certain women's teams and riders that have good support and sponsors, have bigger names, travel to all the races, and get taken care of financially. Even if some of them have day jobs, I'd consider them "pro," even if the team isn't UCI-registered as professional. As long as their bar tape and kit match their name stickers, of course.*

Q **I commute and ride recreationally. I have three kids and a beautiful wife, and the thought of leaving this planet early just scares me. Are there any secrets to increasing motorist awareness of the 3-feet law and a cyclist's rights to the road?**

Man, if you only had two kids and an ugly wife, this wouldn't be such a problem. If there's a secret, no one's told me. I started my online jersey store† hoping to spread the message, or at least feel a little better for trying. If I win the lottery (or sell

---

* A few years later, there are plenty of UCI-registered pro women's teams. Progress!

† Desperate plug. Thank you, *VeloNews*, for allowing it (or putting it in the magazine without reading it).

enough jerseys), I'll buy a Super Bowl ad with responses to every jerk I've ever argued with in traffic: "No, I can't ride on the sidewalk. Yes, I do pay taxes."

My policy for staying on this planet—and I've yet to be hit by anything*—is to assume that not only do the drivers not see me, but they're actually trying to kill me. Don't think that your hunk of flesh and carbon will prevent them from turning right into you if you're in the way when they're late for a hair appointment or trying to beat the morning rush at Starbucks.

Q **When a team sponsor supplies you with components, wheels, clothes, etc., that you personally dislike or don't work for you, how do you feel about keeping a lid on it? Would you still recommend them to consumers?**

Luckily, that's never happened to me.[†] I've been used as a guinea pig for prototypes that never made it to market, and I've used sponsored items I liked more than others,

---

* This streak recently ended when I hit a tractor in Girona. I have a scar, but I'm okay.

† I had to lie here or I'd have been fired. We had water-bottle cages that year that didn't work at all. One pothole would send the bottles flying. I remember being two hours from home and wading into a cold creek in rural Maryland to retrieve two floating bottles that came out on a bridge. We were thirsty in every race, and I had to keep my bottle in my jersey pocket.

especially in the shoe, saddle, and bib-shorts department. For the most part, though, anything that makes its way to the pro ranks or a bike shop works well enough that I'd be happy to recommend it to recreational riders, who generally don't require the same quality or durability as we do.

Hypothetically, if a brand I really hated sponsored my team, my recommendation would depend on who's asking, just how bad the product is, and how good the sponsor is to the team. For example, let's say my team, Kenda, is sponsored by Segway next year, but their contribution is the homicidal scooter they pulled out of the ocean after the company owner tragically rode it off a cliff.* And let's say every time our team director, Frankie Andreu, tries to ride it to registration, it steers him into driving ranges, bear traps, or tall, precarious wedding cakes, and he always has to limp to team appearances with black eyes and stitches, covered in icing. In that case, if my best friend were thinking about spending his year's salary on a new Segway, I'd punch him in the face. On the other hand, what if team manager Chad Thompson told me that the new sponsor is an adult-novelty-toy manufacturer, and that I get to keep one of the team cars they're

---

* This had just been in the news. The joke was widely considered "too soon."

buying us, and my salary is tripled? In that case, if a stranger walked up to me at the start line wearing his bib straps over his T-shirt and asked how it worked, I'd find an extension cord, bend over, and show him.*

Q I noticed that Kenda Pro Cycling went to the Tour de DMZ-Seoul in Korea. As a Korean American cyclist, I've always felt out of place in the pack, so the idea of having entire cycling teams made up of just Koreans is fascinating. What were the Korean riders like over there? Do they all ride 49-cm bikes and XXS clothing, or is it really just me? Also, I'm going to Seoul next month and plan to train while I'm there. What are my chances of becoming roadkill?†

We normally don't do stereotypes here at *VeloNews*, but you started it, and that makes it okay (Martin Luther King Jr. said that in one of his lesser-known speeches). Knowing you, I was surprised to see that the Korean racers were all average-sized. In fact, a few of them were huge and ended

---

* Ewww. They printed that?

† This was from my Korean friend and training partner at the time, Chris Hong, who'd just gotten his first dismal pro contract. We're both sorry about the stereotypes if they offend you, but on the subject of stereotypes, Chris quit racing and went to Harvard, and he's now a doctor. Congrats on your escape, Chris.

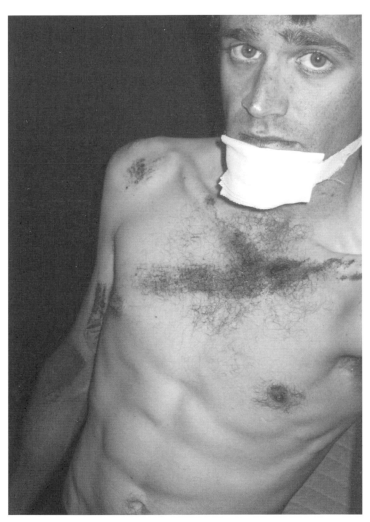

It was the *de*-militarized zone.

up scoring some big results on the track a few weeks after the DMZ Tour. I'd go so far as to say that the "Koreans are small" stereotype is blown out of proportion, if not for an experience at the Seoul airport on the way home. I was sitting in the waiting area with teammate Jake Rytlewski, and we noticed that there were fewer than 30 people lined up for a 100-plus-capacity flight. We rejoiced at the prospect of stretching our legs and reclining, with whole rows to ourselves, when a horrifying sight headed toward our gate: a throng of Korean women, all under 5 feet tall, with identical haircuts and huge shopping bags. The scene was very "Wizard of Oz."

As far as riding in Seoul: The final stage finished in the main square downtown, and I'll never forget the image of Luca Damiani sprinting through traffic because the police were unable to remove the cars from under the finish banner (I was DNFed by then, eating a pizza on the side of the road with bandages on my face). I'd say you should bring a trainer on your trip, but *VeloNews* won't print this for another month, so I assume you're already dead. I offer my condolences to your 5-foot-tall family.*

---

* I've met Chris's family. They're short.

Q **Do you ever find it hard to stay thin? Is it easier when you're racing or when you're training?**

I find it harder to stay skinny when I'm racing, because I'm on the road. You'd think that you can eat whatever you want during multiday races, and while that might be true at the Tour de France, it's not the case at the Nature Valley Grand Prix or USA Crits Speed Week. Often, the races are short or late in the day, leaving you nothing do to but eat in the morning, race for an hour, and eat again before bed. Of course, host moms love to feed you, and you don't want to be rude, so you have 30 to 40 cookies before bed (just to be polite). On the way home, there's a Starbucks every 8 feet at the airport, the chocolate chip banana bread looks pretty good, and you figure you've earned it from all the racing. Then you get to your bathroom scale and have to hit the salads to get back to race weight. It's a vicious cycle, except the cookie part is okay.

Q **After a ride in the rain, I use a paintbrush to wipe away the dirt. Is that a good practice? Is there a better trick?**

I used to make the same mistake. For years, I used various brushes, soaps, and degreasers. They got the bike clean, but it was a lot of work, and I finally stumbled onto a much easier solution. Just be a pro so you can hook your bike onto the rack by the team trailer, forget about it, and go get your massage. It will be magically clean the next day! Sometimes I find a new chain, fresh bar tape, and even full bottles of ice-cold water or drink mix! It's a lot like the tooth fairy: It doesn't make much sense if you think about it, but it always works out.

Q I rode 4 hours today, with 2 × 10–min. tempo efforts at 260 watts, averaging 200 for the whole ride. Is that enough to race as a pro? What kind of numbers do you do on training rides?

First of all, numbers are very relative. If you weigh 60 pounds, those watts will put you in the Tour de France. If you weigh 350, you probably have to walk your bike uphill. Odds are, comparing my numbers to yours won't mean a whole lot.

Second, and more importantly, never show off your numbers like that. Nothing makes a pro cyclist roll his eyes faster than an amateur bragging about power numbers on a blog or Facebook. The power meter is a tool to help you get results, and prize money goes to the first guy across the line, not the guy with the best numbers.

Here's a handy guide to see how it might turn out for you if you publicly announce your power data.*

---

* Someone told me that this chart is on a wall in Quarq's office.

POWER DATA DECISION TREE

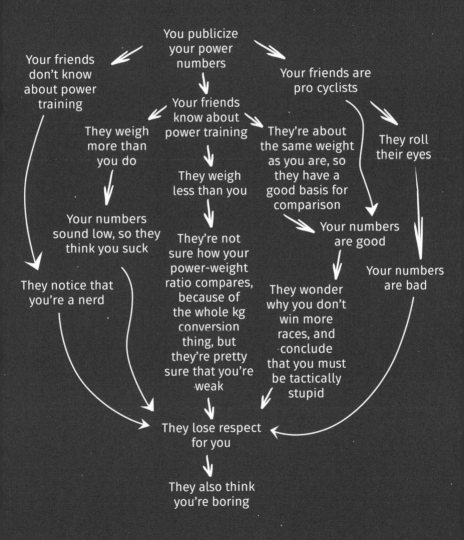

You publicize your power numbers

Your friends don't know about power training

Your friends are pro cyclists

Your friends know about power training

They weigh more than you do

They're about the same weight as you are, so they have a good basis for comparison

They roll their eyes

They weigh less than you

Your numbers sound low, so they think you suck

Your numbers are good

They're not sure how your power-weight ratio compares, because of the whole kg conversion thing, but they're pretty sure that you're weak

Your numbers are bad

They notice that you're a nerd

They wonder why you don't win more races, and conclude that you must be tactically stupid

They lose respect for you

They also think you're boring

If they haven't helped you win races, your power numbers aren't good enough for you to be a pro. If you do win races, that will look better on your résumé than power numbers.*

Q **I've heard that when you're crashing, tucking into a ball is the best way to save your life or prevent serious injury. Is this true? What do you do to protect yourself when you know you're about to crash?**

Bicycles are inherently unstable. I've heard engineers and physicists[†] argue to the contrary, but just take a road bike and try to stand it up by itself in an open area. See? It falls right down. It's a miracle that we stay up at all.

I believe the ancient wise pros do recommend tucking your chin down and holding your arms behind your head. Using your arms to brace a fall is the natural reflex, but it makes you more likely to break a collarbone or a wrist. They say that anything you can do to avoid or minimize impact to the head or spine is advisable.

---

* This is still true. No one has ever gotten a pro contract from a Strava KOM. However, riders have used Strava to convince the team to race them. If you beat Ryder's record up Rocacorba in Girona, you're going to the next race.

† This is a lie. I've never spoken to a physicist.

Intellectually, that makes sense, but in my many experiences of flipping over handlebars, washing out in corners, and being innocently knocked over by incompetents, I've never had time to think about a course of action or take any conscious steps to protect myself. My stages of crash reaction are as follows:

Stage 1: Denial
Stage 2: Screaming profanities

Judging by my history, if I die in a bike race, my last words will almost certainly be four letters at high decibels.

There's only one occasion when I recall anything going through my mind midcrash. It was at the Giro di Jersey in 2009, and the crash happened in slow motion as a wall of riders slid out on wet, slimy roads in front of me. We were descending at low speed, but there still wasn't time to do anything but unclip one foot and tripod toward the pile of bodies.

I remember my train of thought very clearly as I watched the mound of flesh and carbon come closer and closer. First, I gained a sudden appreciation for balance, traction, and low centers of gravity. Then I looked to the side of the road for something softer to aim for, seeing nothing but guardrail, gravel, and empty beer cans. I remember thinking about the guy who drank those beers, probably sitting on the back of a truck with his buddies after a hard day's work. I wondered where I went wrong in my life that the guy who probably didn't go to college or train his butt off to become a pro athlete could drink a beer and toss the can without a care in the world, whereas I was about to limp to CVS to spend $25 on bandages. Then I started screaming profanities. Sorry I can't be of more help.*

Q **I'm one of the best in my area at going uphill. Since you're also a climber, do you have any tips for a guy like me looking to go pro?**

One of the most important things you can learn is that success doesn't like company or competition. If you have the talent to take my job, I would recommend murdering a celebrity in a public place, in broad daylight.

Q **Will you let me win the local race this weekend? I'll give you the prize money, and you've already won a few local races this year, so I need it more than you do.**

---

* I've since learned to aim for something soft. Grass is good.

You know that rush you get when there's no one between you and the finish line, and you realize you've sealed the win in a bike race? I'm Captain Ahab and that feeling is my white whale. I'm an addict for it.* It's also my job to win races, and even if this specific race might not be important to my team, you have to keep sponsors in mind. For example, Masi gives my team a lot of sweet carbon bikes, and they like seeing pictures of me posting up with a view of their fine Italian head badge.

Of course, every man has his price, but by the time you add up the cost of the lost prize money, depriving me of my fix, lost sponsor value, and my dignity and pride (because now there'll be a picture on the Internet of you beating me in a race, along with a text from Frankie Andreu teasing me for it), the price would get a little steep. I'd be embarrassed to look you in the eye and ask for it, and I doubt you'd want to pay it anyway.

But for all concerned, since I don't have to look you in the eye right now, I will take this opportunity to post a pricing system for letting you beat me. (Note: This applies only to small local races, where the prize money for the win is

---

* Only way to break that is cold turkey.

less than $500. I've heard that this totally happens in big races, but I'm in no position to know how that works.)

Base price: $200 + prize money for first place

Add-ons:
+ $150 if you'd like me to act like I'm sprinting you at the end
+ $200 if you'd like to win solo
+ $100 if I don't like you

Discounts:
– $50 if I do like you
– $50 if I'm hurting for gas money
– $50 if you can supply a paper bag with eyeholes cut out for the podium pictures, so no one will recognize me

Oh. Cash only.*

---

* I never sold a race. I did let David Guttenplan win once. We were team-mates and it was just the two of us left in the breakaway. I asked him if he'd let me have it. "Well, my parents are here," he said, so it was his. He would have easily outsprinted me anyway.

Q We all know how idiotic, and even disdainful, drivers can be with us bikers. What do you say to someone if they honk or almost hit you?

The more you ride, the more angry drivers you inevitably encounter. In many areas, the worst thing you can do is give the middle finger. In New York City, that's as normal as a handshake, but in central Florida, it sends rednecks into an irrational rage, like the guy who nearly flipped his minivan while buzzing us at Kenda's training camp, or a man I encountered in north Georgia. He was so frustrated at the slight delay I caused him, he honked and spewed diesel fumes at me, but when he saw my raised finger, his busy schedule freed up, and he found enough time to stop, pull a chain out of his truck, and threaten to show me "where to put that finger, boy!" I told him I was sincerely sorry, and he left me unharmed.

If you're able to catch up and talk to them, some drivers are actually apologetic and receptive to reason. Tell them how to be safe and thank them for listening. Others just start yelling right away. For them, if a witty insult comes to mind in time, shame is always a powerful weapon, and I've had some success making fun of the driver's appearance, car, bumper stickers, etc. For example, if a middle-aged man yells at you from his small convertible, you can say, "Relax,

Share the road, but obey traffic signs even when they don't make sense.

I didn't scratch your wife's car." Or if a young woman who looks like she's had a long night stops to cuss at you: "I'm just doing my job. I don't go to where you work and tell you how to wear your G-string."* If that doesn't work out for you, a good go-to response is a friendly wave and a smile. The sarcasm is satisfying, and it won't get your finger put anywhere uncomfortable.

Q What is the best way to get a job on a pro cycling team? As a driver, bike mechanic, whatever . . .

Pro teams are tough to crack as a rider, but it might be tougher as staff, since there are even fewer jobs and likely similar competition. I'm guessing you don't have the contacts if you're asking me here, so my advice would be to be proactive about it, like Kenda-5-Hour Energy-Geargrinder's mechanic, Will Swan.

Will learned to wrench at a bike shop and decided he wanted to be a pro mechanic, so he signed up for a class from Park Tool. When he told his classmates that he wanted to work for a pro team, they laughed, but he e-mailed someone through a website, volunteered his services to Kenda as assistant mechanic, and proved a good guy and a hard

---

* She was pissed.

worker. He's now Kenda's head mechanic, no longer taking his pay only in beer.*

Two pieces of advice:

1. Don't try to take Will's job. He looks docile, but he can kill you with his bare hands in dozens of different ways.

2. If you do land a job on a pro team, riders like me will ask to borrow tools. If we ask for your 5-mm Allen wrench, hold on to it like Charlton Heston clutched his Winchester ("from my cold, dead hands!").

Q Do you eat scrapple?

I've spent a few summers in eastern Pennsylvania, which is prime scrapple country. At least once every year, I looked at the menu at a diner, realized I'd forgotten what scrapple was exactly, and then looked it up to learn (again) that it's literally random, compressed pig parts, mushed into a loaf, and then fried, making it probably one of the worst things

---

* Being qualified and willing to work for free is the key to any job.

you can put into your body. I'm sure you've heard the term "pizza legs," referring to how bad you feel at a race if you ate pizza the night before. I don't want to imagine what "scrapple legs" are like, and I think it's good policy for your stomach to avoid any food with the word "crap" right in the name. That said, one of my mottos is that two out of three people suffer from diarrhea, and the other one enjoys it, so if you want to try it, it's up to you to learn which category you fall into.

Q How do you stay motivated day in and day out? I love racing and riding, but sometimes the training gets monotonous.

It's true, you can have too much of a good thing. Imagine a male adult-film star, who just got home from a long day of "work." His beautiful wife is in the mood, and he'd love to, but he just doesn't feel like it. That's how we all feel about riding sometimes.

When motivation dips, it helps to have an iPod, some good riding partners, or a change of scenery. Try trading the road bike for a mountain bike, or go stay with a friend in another city and ride some new roads. If you're not a pro, don't forget you can take some time off for a mental break, and no one will blame you for it.

As for me, I love every minute of it. if somone offrd me a nillion follars to chande jobs, I'd necer tsake it. [Editor: Sorru anout typos. It's hard ti type eith fingerd crossed.]

Q I see a lot of pro riders tweeting about getting their bikes onto a plane for free. How do they do it, and why do they bother? Don't their teams pay for that anyway?

Credit goes to Jeremy Powers for sparking the Airport Ninja* movement. No guarantees that you can avoid the fees, but I can tell you a few things to watch out for when packing your bike.

1. *Weight:* Your box must be under 50 pounds, or they'll charge you for overweight baggage. Weigh it on your scale at home and pack heavier parts in your other bag if necessary. I once found myself taking random parts out of the bike box and throwing them into my carry-on at check-in to reduce the weight. I ended up at security wielding a set of SRAM Red cranks with chainrings attached. True story: They ignored this formidable weapon and confiscated my iced tea.

---

* He regrets not trademarking this term.

2. *Size:* There are certain size limits to your bike box, varying by airline, and the mood and generosity of whoever's measuring. Remove the cranks, seatpost, fork, etc., so the bike can fit in the smallest box possible.

3. *It must not look like a bike:* If you showed up with a 5-pound shoebox and told them it was a bike, you could be charged the general "bike fee," which should be illegal, especially with all the golf club bags that go through for free. (Are any lawyers reading this? I see class-action lawsuit potential.)* To beat this one, make sure your box isn't covered in bike-related stickers, there's no helmet dangling from your backpack, etc. If they ask what's in it, go with "trade show display" or my favorite: "just a bunch of crap." Despite this subterfuge, sometimes you can get everything right, but when you get to the airport you discover the guy at the counter just got dumped by his girlfriend and is making himself feel better by playing God with your wallet (I once had to pay oversized, overweight, and a separate bike fee). In that case, you either pay

---

* No response to this plea. Apparently, lawyers do not read *VeloNews.*

whatever he demands and call customer service later for a refund, or you miss your flight.

Personally, I have trouble getting my 61-cm frame under the size restrictions and rarely slip my bike onto a flight for free. I have lots of bikes, so I usually take the cop-out route and mail it before I leave.

As far as who pays for it, that depends on the team, the budget, and so on, but even if the team was paying, that's $150 I'd rather have them spend on champagne after a win than flying my bike around, so I still go ninja (although security doesn't appreciate people wearing ninja masks).

Overall, the airlines are constantly changing their rules and finding new ways to charge you, like $25 for a carry-on and $5 for off-brand trail mix. I predict that in 10 years, having run out of fees for "extras," they'll actually charge you if you don't want to sit in the "duct tape class" (where they strap you to the fuselage), or flight attendants will roam the aisles, hitting passengers with a cane if they haven't paid the $25 "no-beatings" fee.*

---

* Original version of this joke was a device that came out of the seat cushion up your ass unless you feed quarters into the armrest to retract it.

Q **Is there anything you've learned in racing that you'll apply to the outside world or in an office someday? What will you take away from cycling when you retire?**

For the most part, being able to pedal fast probably won't look great on a résumé, but there are a few skills that translate.

1. Playing hurt. In a big race, if you're suffering from illness, scrapes, bruises, or injury, you have the attitude that they'll have to peel your rotting corpse off your bike before you quit, and dumb stoicism like that applies anywhere. Remember when Tyler Hamilton finished the Tour de France with his broken collarbone? If he ends up at a desk job, do you think he'd call in sick if he got a bad case of the sniffles?*

2. Professional cyclists are the best drivers in the world, except for professional drivers. We drive fast, we're good at staying attentive for extended periods, and racer instincts keep us safe. Also, we learn to save energy by avoiding accelerations and conserving

---

* He'd blame Lance Armstrong and have someone ghostwrite a tell-all book about it.

momentum, and that leads to good gas-management habits, like coasting up to stoplights instead of using gas and brakes.

3. Mostly, what I'll take away are experiences: good times, places I've been, and things I've seen. I've raced across the Golden Gate Bridge, and I've climbed around the Tibetan Plateau. Once, on a training ride in my own town, I even saw a unicorn (it might have been a goat with one horn broken off).

Those memories will be with me the rest of my life, as long as I don't crash on my head and forget them. What was the question, again?

Q My husband has bikes and bike stuff everywhere, and he only rides recreationally. How many bikes do you have, and how many do you need?

Cycling is an equipment-intensive sport. I think I'm up to eight bikes,* and I can say with a straight face that I need all of

---

* Not anymore. As a WorldTour rider, I don't own my bikes. These days I'm down to two bikes that actually belong to me, and one is a 1979 Miyata steel thing I take to the grocery store.

them. It's my job, though, so that doesn't necessarily mean that your husband needs that many. Does a guy who likes to doodle in Microsoft Paint need the same computer as a graphic designer? I think a good number of cyclists are more interested in collecting the gear as a hobby than actually using it, so it might be less about how good of a rider he is, and more about how much he enjoys spending time on rubbing his frames down with VeloShine.* Overall, your husband's bike needs depend on whether you can afford it, and if you're a good wife or not. If you love him, you'll work harder and encourage him to quit his job so he can play with his 20 bikes full-time. Does he have a nice town bike yet? Masi's Soulville[†] has internal gearing, cork grips, and a lovely paint scheme.

As far as space is concerned, I live in an apartment, so my training bike has a permanent home standing in the corner near the door, and the rest of the bikes hang on the wall. I'm good about getting rid of old stuff I won't need anymore and keeping my tools and parts impeccably neat (although I'm a complete slob in most aspects of my life), so it's reasonable to expect the same of your husband.

---

* Blatant sponsor plug.

† Geez, another one, but look how smooth I am. You'd never have noticed. I do like that bike.

Sometimes, my girlfriend (who doesn't ride bikes) will find a grease stain somewhere unexpected, like the inside of the refrigerator. I can't explain that, I refuse to clean it, and I resent the implication that I might have caused it.*

Q Do all cyclists have agents like other sports?

I think most of the top-level Euro pros do have agents. They help to make sure you get a good contract and little extras you might need, like the famous bowl of M&Ms with the brown ones removed. An agent prevents the awkwardness of haggling with your future boss, but they do charge a fee (typically 5 to 10 percent of your salary), so lower-level guys usually can't afford it, and agents wouldn't find it worth their time. For most domestic riders, that would be like a homeless person who sells dreamcatchers on the side of the road looking to hire a lawyer.

Q I saw you on TV, trying to make the breakaway at the Tour of California, but the HTC team was blocking the road. What are the rules on pushing someone out of your

---

* That relationship did not last.

way when they do that? I would have treated those HTC boys like bowling pins, and just explained that their white jerseys confused me. Are those guys A-holes?

The rules are unwritten and full of gray areas, but mostly formed out of respect. Small teams like mine all want to be in the break for their sponsors, but the big teams want the break to be small so they have an easier time chasing it down. When the leader's jersey stops to pee (I don't think it's a coincidence that the leader wears yellow), that's the indication that the break can go, the race usually neutralizes, and the lower guys respect it.

In the case you saw on TV, HTC blocked the road so a break could go, and no Kenda riders were in the move. It was much too late to get across, but I elbowed and squeezed through and got off the front for a bit, mostly because I was angry, yelling, "excuse me, pardon me," until they made room. There was some bumping, but as long as I kept my hands on the bars and didn't cause any crashes, no one could really get angry about it. The attack itself got me yelled at and made fun of, but I'm prepared to handle that. It was the last stage of our biggest race of the year, we have our own job to do, and they were abusing their yellow-jersey privileges.

It doesn't make them A-holes, because intimidation is a legitimate tactic. It often works, and it's their responsibility to do whatever they can to save their legs. I've done the same to amateurs at smaller races, and if the tables were turned, I'd probably have acted much like the European teams did at the Tour of California.* When I got caught, most of them respected my motivation, but a few still had rude things to say. Those are the A-holes.

Q What do you do when you're selected for a race you don't like? Who decides which riders go to each race?

The team director chooses the best roster for each race, factoring in everyone's form, fitness, and abilities. Usually, the riders like the races that they're well suited for, so it works out. Often, there are too many riders who want to go to a certain race, and someone has to miss out. There are occasions, though, when the team is short a guy, or someone gets injured and you have to take their spot, or you just finished a long block of racing and want to go home. When that happens, it comes down to doing what your boss says or risk getting fired. If there's a specific race that I really

---

* They have been, and I did.

don't want to go to, that's something I'd have to bring up at contract time. For example, my contract states that if I have to race the notoriously crash-heavy Athens Twilight Criterium, Kenda is required to equip me with old car tires, which I'll drape over myself with rope like a tugboat.*

Q I'm interested in getting on your team next year. Where do I send my résumé?[†]

You should send it right to the trash can. Actually, I take that back. I apologize. I want you to recycle it.

Q I'd like to know about tire pressure. It seems like 120 psi is the standard for road racing. Is that what you use in all conditions? If not, how do you decide what pressure to put in? Do you factor in rolling resistance?

Riders adjust tire pressure to different conditions, but the biggest factor is rider weight. The more you weigh, the higher you need to go, so a 120-lb. rider might race with 100 psi, while a 175-lb. rider would shoot for 125 or 130.

---

* Should have done this for Paris-Roubaix.

† If it's annoying that I answered this question multiple times in the column, just imagine how often people ask me in real life.

If the course is wet, unpaved, or technical, your pressure should go down, so you need to do a little homework to get it right.*

I used to nerd out and think about the courses, rolling resistance, and optimal tire pressure, until the team signed Ben Day. Ben is a supernerd, with notes so detailed he can tell you if he big-ringed the steep parts when he won the Redlands prologue. Having Ben around has really cut down my personal homework load, because I've instituted the "Whatever Ben's having" policy. It's like when Burger King wants to open a new store. They don't want to spend the money and time to research the best locations, factoring in the cost of real estate, foot traffic, competition, and so on, and McDonald's has already done that research. So what does Burger King do? They open a store next to the McDonald's. In this analogy, I consider myself the Burger King, and Ben the McDonald's. When the soigneur asks if I want a massage, I ask, "Did Ben get one?" This applies to almost everything, including tire pressure, whether I use the deep or shallow Mercury wheels, Pomegranate 5-Hour Energy or Grape, skim

* Crazy how much this has changed. I'm 150 pounds and race at 105–110 psi now. Less with wider tires and rims. Don't follow my advice on this—or anything.

milk or 2 percent. You get the idea. You might call it lazy, but I call it efficiency. If you can get his phone number, I highly recommend the "Whatever Ben's having" policy.* For the record, he's married, so I wouldn't apply it to his personal life.

Q I notice riders pinning the number 13 on upside-down for good luck. Are all pros superstitious? What other traditions are there like that?

The one time I pinned a number 13 on upside-down, I ended up sliding into the barricades on it, and a spectator stole my favorite sunglasses (they had the photochromatic lenses, and I want them back). One could argue that maybe I was fated to decapitate myself in that crash, and the minor road rash was in fact good luck, but I don't buy into any of that crap anymore.

There are two other universal superstitions in cycling that I widely ignore, to the despair and shock of friends and teammates, and I will take this opportunity to further challenge the gods of bike racing. Superstition is stupid.

Superstition No. 1: Don't point out that it's been awhile since you crashed.

---

* Appropriately, Ben is a coach now.

Tempting Fate: I haven't hit the deck since the Tour de DMZ-Seoul in October 2010. When I do crash, it will not be because I mentioned it here. It will be because I either did something stupid or rode behind someone who did something stupid.

Superstition No. 2: Don't point out that it's been awhile since you flatted.

Tempting Fate: Of course, if you're on Kenda tires, you don't have to worry about it very much, but my last flat was in mid-June during the final stage of the Tour de Beauce, when teammate Bobby Sweeting led me up the outside of the field directly into a giant sewer-drain hole. Do we blame fate for that? I blame Bobby Sweeting 45 percent, poor Canadian road maintenance 45 percent, myself (and I'm being generous here) 5 percent, and my high school math teachers 15 percent.

Aside from those major superstitions, I think a lot of riders have evolved their own personal routines for good luck. For example, Chad Hartley punched a teammate in the crotch before the start of the Univest Criterium in 2004. He won the race, so now he starts every race by punching a teammate in the crotch, for good luck. Or maybe he's just a jerk.

As I said, I don't have any issues like that. I do bring a rubber chicken to most races, which some people assume is for good luck, but Deborah is merely a low-maintenance, travel-friendly pet who encourages me to pedal harder, and I won't have you trivialize her role in my success.*

Q **I'm trying to figure out what kind of rider I am. What determines whether a pro is a sprinter, climber, or time trialist? Is it what they train for, what they like most, or what they're naturally better at?**

Your question is basically the old nature-versus-nurture debate. I'd guess that the answer boils down to genetics. If you're 5 feet tall, 90 pounds, with big lungs and slow-twitch muscles, no matter how much you like sprinting and train for it, you're going to suck. Folks enjoy rides where they can beat their friends, and then they're more motivated to train those strengths. For example, I'm tall, skinny, and slow-twitch. My coach can throw sprint intervals at me all he wants, but I'll never be good at it.

---

* I've lost Deborah, and I have no feelings about it.

There's also a mental aspect to your rider type. I've known some guys with fast-twitch genes that spout massive sprint power on the group ride but don't have what it takes (or, more likely, are missing a crucial part of their brain) to do something crazy in the last turn to win the crit. Our team field sprinter, Isaac Howe, is mentally and physically gifted for field sprinting. I once snuck up behind him and yelled "boo!" while he was watching TV. The guy didn't even flinch.

If you want to determine what type of rider you are, sign yourself up for a hard race and see if you get dropped on climbs, flats, or surging, technical sprinty parts. Wherever you get dropped most, you're the other kind of rider.

Q **I went to the start of a stage at the Amgen Tour of California this year. I didn't know any of the riders personally, but I was surprised to find them very approachable and friendly, especially compared to other sports. Why is that?**

You like bike racing, but that puts you in the minority. Most pros realize that no matter how famous, well-paid, or fast you are, 99 percent of the world considers you an inconvenience that needs to get the hell out of the road, and they can't tell the Tour de France from a gay pride parade. They see a few seconds on TV every year of dudes wearing colorful tights, crashing in France, and think "That's a sport?" So when we encounter a true fan, we like to chat, because it makes up for all the rednecks who throw beer cans at us.

Q I have a question concerning the most important member of all pro-cycling teams: the soigneur. Why do most teams require them to wash the riders' laundry every day? Do you just bring one kit to a 10-day bike race? And also, do you really think that they don't notice that you've stuffed underwear in your laundry bag in the hopes that they don't see it?

(I should first inform readers that this question came from a real-life pro soigneur, which is the massage therapist/feeder that travels with a team. One of their duties during stage races is laundry, which the riders leave outside their rooms in mesh bags after the stages.)*

I'm not sure why teams require daily laundry. I bring at least three kits to most races, so I only need laundry done

---

* The clothes are washed and dried within the mesh bags so they don't get mixed up, but this soigneur had a weird thing where she didn't like our underwear being in there. I tried to explain to her here that she was being unreasonable, but I was careful not to piss her off, because she worked for my team sometimes.

once or twice a week. Unless the weather is nasty, and we've dirtied up our only pair of arm or leg warmers, I don't see why anyone would need it daily. I think this is a valid point that you could bring up with team management and riders.

However, you should make a concession on the under-wear thing. I would say that the average American changes underwear and T-shirts daily, especially if they're crammed in cars or buses after a race. Are we expected to bring seven shirts and pairs of underwear when we're getting our riding clothes washed anyway? I change my underwear at least once a week, whether I need to or not, and you wouldn't want to share a dinner table or give a massage to anyone who didn't. You should be relieved that your riders want clean underwear.

Q What's the best way to lose weight and stay lean? What's the worst way?

I think the only way to lose it and keep it off is to change your lifestyle to be more active and to eat healthier. The whole idea of going on a diet implies that you plan to go off it, and the weight will come back. Read ingredients and nutrition info, find what healthy foods work for you, have a little willpower, and get into a routine with it. Once it's part of your regular

pattern, healthy eating isn't so hard. The more gradually you make these changes, the more likely they are to stick.

The worst way to lose weight is to crash on your face and have to get your jaw wired shut. But if you sign a waiver and send me $500, I'd be glad to break it myself with my fist.

Q **What's the best victory celebration? Is it something you practice? Do most riders have a "signature" move?**

The proper victory celebration is whatever comes from your gut at the moment of victory. It's emotional, sincere, and almost involuntary. I find it pretty tacky if someone has anything too elaborate or "signature." I roll my eyes when Contador does the *pistolero* thing. The only exception is the victory canoe, where you paddle across the line. That one is awesome.

If you can ride with your hands off the bars, there's no reason to practice. I'd be horrified that someone will see me. There's no way to play off the victory canoe.

Q **What do you use to lube your chain? What's the point of those expensive bike lubes? I just use WD-40, and I've never had a problem.**

Why would you lube your chain with a tax form?

Q **What do you do to get enough calories in stage races?**

It can be tough to replenish all the energy your body uses up in some of the longer stages. The race usually provides a buffet, which is a good start. As the race progresses, I think most riders shoot higher up the food pyramid, to the tastier/less healthy food groups, just because we're sick of eating pasta. My salad at dinner will have less lettuce and more croutons and cheese every day (by the end, it's just a ranch-dressing soup). Aside from that, there's a lot of snacking. I'm a fan of rice cakes with peanut butter or honey. Teammate Jim Stemper never stops eating cereal. We're looking into a feedbag sponsor so he can just wear it on his face like a horse.

Q **How should I explain my shaved legs to girls? Do you shave yours year-round, or only during the racing season?**

You don't owe them any explanation. Instead, explain why they should thank you: Besides the fact that your legs are muscular and beautiful, male cyclists' familiarity with our own leg stubble makes the girl's life easier. If I go three days without shaving my legs, they feel like sandpaper. Since girl hair is finer, my girlfriend could go a month without shaving hers before I even notice.*

I keep my legs shaved year-round.† I always try the lazy route in the off-season, but I can never fight through that itchy/prickly phase when you first let it go, so I'm forced into this perpetual losing battle. I'd say about half the pros I know let their leg hair grow in the off-season. The day before photo shoots at training camp, everyone busts out the buzzers (some teams actually have communal buzzers), and the poor maid at the hotel must have a horrible time the next day, having to clean up what looks like some sort of fetish party in every room.

---

* I like that I've tackled this question before, but the answer is different.

† WorldTour riders pretty much only shave before races. I'm down to once a week these days.

Q I have a question about a guy who comes on the local group ride. He's strong and could easily do it on a road bike, but he rides a TT bike with tubulars and all sorts of high-end gear. He doesn't ride in his aerobars in the pack, but he runs lights, and when there's a breakaway, he'll go to the front and chase it down. He can't sprint, so he rarely wins, but he nullifies any attacks with these efforts, and when he does stay away solo, he has elaborate victory celebrations. How do we deal with this guy?

Group rides have no official rules or leaders, but they are a competition, especially for non-racer types, and the playing field should be somewhat level. Sure it's just a TT bike, but what if someone shows up with a motorcycle? Complaining makes you look pathetic, so you're really in a lose-lose situation. As long as he's not putting anyone in danger, I don't think there's anything you can or should do about it.

Just past anger, though, is empathy: I think you're focusing too much on his riding style, and not enough on the years of emotional and physical abuse this man must have been put through to turn into such a pain in the butt. You're not born with that much of a chip on your shoulder. If victory on a group ride means that much to someone, they've already lost anywhere it counts in life. He's probably been fired and divorced over and over. I recommend you swallow your pride and let this guy have his one victory.

Q **These Occupy Wall Street protests are all over the news. As a pro cyclist, are you in the 1 percent? How much money do you make?**

I probably make less than you do. But I get free bikes, clothes, and sunglasses, and my name is embroidered on my luggage. You can't put a price on that. What? You can get your name embroidered on most anything for a nominal surcharge? Shit.

Q **How did you get where you are?**

Let's start at the beginning. Billions of years ago (although time is relative), all the matter in the universe was condensed into a tiny point. It had infinite mass and density, and no volume, so it popped, and . . . I think I'm going to run out of space in this one, so let's skip ahead a little. Caesar crossed the Rubicon, Albert Einstein invented electricity, and I rode my bike a lot so that I had a better power-to-weight ratio than most people. Does that make sense? If it does, you should see a doctor.

Q How much time do you take off the bike in the winter, and what do pro cyclists do for crosstraining?

Most pros take at least two weeks completely off the bike, and some might take up to a couple months, depending on their fitness at the end of the season, whether they had any injuries, and when their first race will be in the next season. How they choose to spend their "me time" varies just as widely. My team director, Frankie Andreu, used to sign up for a winter basketball league. (I think they used a ball of twine and a wicker peach basket back then.) Ben Day and Frank Pipp have been talking trash about a tennis match.* (How much would you pay to watch that?) Some of my New England friends, like Shawn Milne and Jeremy Powers, do this thing called psychocross, which, judging from the pictures, appears to be a form of sponsored mud wrestling.

I've always finished my season with a race in Asia and a 15-hour flight, so I get home and announce that I'm not touching a bike for a month. I then sleep 12-hour nights for a week, wake up itchy to ride again, and force myself to at least take another week off. For crosstraining, I stick

---

* Alex Howes and Kiel Reijnen tried to have a boxing match once, but their contracts didn't allow it.

to gym work (so men with upper-body muscles can laugh at me), and last year, my coach had me add plyometrics, which might have been an attempt to kill me. This routine took place in various snow-covered parks in Baltimore (where they wouldn't find the body until February), started with explosive lunges, and finished with picnic-table jumps. Take a look at a regular picnic table, and ask yourself if you could jump up on top of it. The first time I went, I didn't know either, but I took a (literal) leap of faith and made it, barely. I did 10 picnic-table jumps in a row that day and added 2 each time with no issues, until the last week, when I'd built up to 30. On number 28, my feet slipped off, my shins scraped down the edge of the cement table, and I army-crawled back to the car, leaving a trail of blood in the snow. What was the question? How I got those scars on my shins?

Q When I'm riding in heavy traffic, I often run red lights. I feel like it's safer, because it lets me claim my lane before I'll have to fight cars for it. Have you observed the same thing? Do pros run lights? What about four-way stops? I want to obey the laws, but it seems like everybody runs through them.

I wouldn't say that I run red lights, but I also treat them as four-way stops. In my experience, if you're next to the cars when the light turns green, they're very likely to squeeze you into the curb once you've crossed the intersection. If you see a safe gap in traffic and get a head start, you're risking a ticket, but you're less likely to get run over or punted onto the sidewalk, and what's more important? I'll jump the light every time.

I also run the light or the four-way stop if I'm out in the country and I can see that nobody's there. Yes, it's illegal, but as cyclists, we have to keep our heads on a swivel at all times and constantly watch out for vehicles that might not see us. The upside of our forced paranoia is that we're acutely aware of our surroundings, and I think that entitles us to a few liberties. Cosmically, it just makes us even for all the times we've been cut off or forced into the grass. I can't legally advocate breaking the law, but if you look around and can see it's safe to go, don't let The Man tell you otherwise. This is America, and sometimes you have to toss the tea into the harbor. I'm Phil Gaimon, and I approved this message.*

---

* Don't sue me. Remember, if you're a lawyer reading this, sue the airlines on my behalf instead.

Q How do you stay away from unhealthy foods when you're trying to watch your weight? It seems like every time I go on a diet, somebody bakes brownies, and it's hard to resist.

I've also noticed the phenomenon of food magically appearing when I'm trying to be careful. I once decided to lose a few pounds, and I was immediately crushed by a cake that fell from the sky. When someone wants to bake at my house, I force them to make something I don't like (such as cookies with butterscotch chips), and then I demand they cough on the tray as soon as it comes out of the oven.

Q I have some questions about drug testing. You hear a lot about frequent testing of guys like Lance and Cavendish. Are domestic pros tested constantly as well? Have you ever missed a test, or had any fears that your test would be positive? What's the procedure like?

Domestic pros are tested, but not as often as the bigger names. At NRC races, UCI races, and national championships, they usually test the winner and one or two random riders in the field. I've been tested at races several times, and I've twice received the dreaded e-mail from USADA informing me that they'll need to know my whereabouts every hour for the next year for out-of-competition testing. When I was in that testing pool, there were long periods where I wouldn't be tested at all, and others where I was tested so frequently that I'd have trouble urinating if someone in a white lab coat wasn't watching.

I did miss a test once, sort of. If you live in an apartment, you're supposed to include instructions with your where-abouts sheet on how to enter the building. The tester saw the buzzer and the keypad (both of which were broken) and never actually tried the door, which would have opened easily. When I woke up to six missed calls between 6 and 7 a.m., I panicked, but you don't get in trouble until you've missed three tests within 12 months, and it never happened again. After a bunch of e-mails, they took it off my record.

I was never too worried about a test going positive, but every time the guy leaves, you can't help but think about every roadside taco, piece of steak, or chimera twin you might have consumed. As a founder of the clean tattoo club, if I ever dope or test positive, there's a pact that the other members of the club will show up at my house and remove my tattoo with a cheese grater, so there's more to lose than my reputation. So far, so good.

The dope-testing procedure is strict and official. Every-thing is packed and sealed in foam and shrink-wrap, and you open it yourself, so you don't worry about tampering or contamination. You sign some forms, inspect the equipment, and match codes on the bottles to codes on the sheet and the package to prevent a mix-up. Then you go to the bathroom, where some stranger watches you pee into a cup, and it's not like you put your back to him. He has to watch it come out of you, and he stares. I don't know where they find these people. Once you've filled the cup, you pour it into the two sample bottles, seal it all up into a jar that locks so it that can't be reopened, finish filling out the forms, and then beg your roommates* to stop laughing at you.

Q It takes me forever to get a new bike or parts into the position I want, especially cleats. Is this normal? Are there are any tricks to getting it right?

Position can be very frustrating. The more I ride, the more I turn into the Princess and the Pea when it comes to this sort of thing. When I got back from training camp last year, my training bike was matched perfectly to the race bike I had just gotten used to, but I could tell that someone had left the pedal

---

* Only fair since the doorbell probably woke them up at 6 a.m.

washers on, and I had to ride back to my house to remove them before I started my intervals.

If there are any foolproof tricks, I don't know them, but I do have some tips that might help. First, use the same cloth tape to measure everything. Also, try to stick to the same equipment as much as possible, and use the same saddles and bars on all your bikes. Remember that certain brands are easier to adjust and fine-tune than others. Trust your instincts: If it feels wrong, it is. Lastly, if you're going to ride on something new, don't bring any friends, because if you need to stop and fix it, they won't want to wait for you.

Q Congrats on your wins in San Dimas and Redlands.* Do you have any advice for an uphill time trial I'm signed up for? My bike is light. I race and train with power and know roughly what wattage I can hold for about 10 minutes, the likely duration. I also have a good 60-minute warm-up routine.

My question: Is there any advantage to alternating sitting and standing, spinning at an above-average cadence, attacking the hill two or three times within the TT? Or is it

---

* I won things!

best to simply get up to speed and then stare at my power meter? Also, I'm 6 feet 1 inches, 160 lb., Category III—should I try to lose weight?

Me winning something.

Pacing should always depend on terrain. In any time trial, you should save the most energy for the hardest parts; for an uphill TT, that's the steepest portions. I think cadence is mostly a preference, but I always feel more powerful when I'm spinning high RPMs and seated. I only stand up to accelerate back to speed after a steep pitch or a corner that slows me down.

When it comes to weight, as an amateur riding for Fiordifrutta in 2008, I found myself at a group ride in Boulder, where I overheard some of the best domestic climbers (who shall remain nameless) talking about negative-calorie soup and how skinny they got themselves in the winter. "I got to 135 before I got sick," bragged one of my manorexic idols. That comment stuck in my mind. You're in for a long career if you want to be a climber.

It's a sad reality that the skinnier you are, the better you go uphill, as long as you don't get to the point that you're wasting away and your power suffers. I recently saw a starving child in an African relief commercial and slapped myself for wondering how he got so lean. I do enjoy the simplicity of a job that boils down to a power-to-weight ratio, but you have to keep an eye on it so you don't shut down your metabolism and make yourself sick.

Pick the races where it's most crucial to be skinny, lose the weight slowly, and let it come back afterward. Get periodic skinfold tests to keep track of your body composition. Never go below 4 percent.

If you're still a Cat. III, you don't have to put yourself through that yet. Just get stronger and grab those upgrade points. There's nothing more annoying than a Cat. III who drives his friends nuts walking around in compression tights and weighing his food, and it doesn't make sense for you to make those sacrifices. Don't skip the brownies until losing the extra five pounds will actually affect your life. And for the love of God, don't start brewing negative-calorie soup. A friend once pulled out a scale to weigh his pasta at my house. I told him to put it away or we'd see how much his front teeth weighed.

Q I always name my bikes. Do you ever get attached to a bike? Do you give them names?

When I toured Masi's warehouse in California, I met a bike named Vincere Bellissima.* We rode away together, but it wasn't meant to be, and I don't like to talk about it.

---

* This was their women's frame. The first draft had a part where I removed the seat, and it got graphic.

Q **I was thinking about getting weekly massages for recovery, but the whole idea is weird to me. Is it awkward to get a massage as a male?**

The first time I got a massage, it was hard to get over the concept that another human being was being paid to rub me. Who am I? Cleopatra? But it does really help, and everybody does it, so you get over it quickly. Halfway through, when they tell you to flip over onto your belly, ask to use the restroom and smear your rear end with Nutella. Never gets old.

Q **I'm not a professional, but I try to take my training seriously. Part of that, as you know, is getting proper recovery. But when I get home from a ride, my wife doesn't understand why I don't want to mow the lawn. She also makes fun of me for watching my weight and diet, using a power meter, and so on. How can I convey the importance of these things to a non-athlete?**

The first thing that crosses my mind when I read your question is, "He'd better be real fast, or this guy is a huge pain in the ass." Imagine if your wife became obsessed with fast cars, then started spending thousands of dollars buying new parts and upgrades and hours installing them. You'd wonder if it was worth the time and money she was investing. But if she started winning races, you'd be proud and give her some space. However, if she went through all that and then drove exactly the speed limit in the right lane with her blinker on all day, getting honked at, you'd have a right to complain.

If you're getting in shape and doing reasonably well, and she sees that you're accomplishing something, she'll eventually come to respect the sacrifice it takes. But if you're just having fun attacking your buddies on the group ride, mix up a recovery drink, grab a sandwich, and bust out the lawn mower when you get home. Then come over and mow my lawn, because my recovery is important.

Q **I'm 18 years old. I've been training hard for a couple of years now, watching my diet (I'm still a little overweight), and generally doing my best, but I'm still a weak Cat. IV. I've come to the conclusion that I'm just not talented. Does success always come to those who put in the work, or is there something genetic that you have to be born with?**

I have to say I admire your honesty. Most people would have trouble admitting that they're overweight, weak, and untalented. As good as it is to accept your weaknesses, don't sound so sad. I half expected a P.S. to explain that you're not too bright, you have horrible acne, and your breath stinks.

I do believe that success comes to those who put in the work. Being born with talent doesn't hurt, but my parents are college professors, not athletic at all, and I've achieved a level of success despite that.

Of course, genes are a factor, so if Taylor Phinney—whose parents were both world-class cyclists—is on the far right of the bell curve, and I'm somewhere in the middle, it is possible that you could be on the far left and have no talent. My advice would be to race as much as you can, and set goals one step at a time (becoming a Cat. III, for example). If you do have less talent than your competitors, use that to give yourself a little anger in your training. Worst-case scenario? You'll learn to work hard to get ahead, and that will pay off when you do find something you're good at. Keep that in mind when you get too down on yourself, but just in case, go brush your teeth.

Q Is it true that power-meter manufacturers will be including antidepressants with new orders?

That's just a rumor at this point. I have been testing a new product for Quarq that adjusts itself based on weight and rider type. I'm a climber, so for me, it spews confetti when I break 1,300 watts.

Q **What do pros think when they see a recreational cyclist outfitted in a full pro kit or riding a pro version bike?**

Wait a minute. Are you saying that recreational cyclists can just buy the same kits and bikes that pros get? This explains why Jan Ullrich looked so fat the other day when I ran into him. I thought he'd just let himself go, and I had definitely expected more of an accent and less of an attitude.*

Q **What can I do off the bike to boost my watts, and what off-the-bike activities might be slowing me down?**

Everyone talks about intervals or training to improve power, or weight loss to improve power-to-weight ratios, but off-the-bike factors are easily overlooked and can make a big difference. From my years of experience as an athlete and a coach, I've put together a chart on the next page of a few activities that can help or harm your ride the next day.

---

* This is a big problem in Los Angeles. In Girona, it's often the opposite. "Look at that guy with the full Etixx . . . oh, hey Marcel!"

WATTS HOLDING YOU BACK?

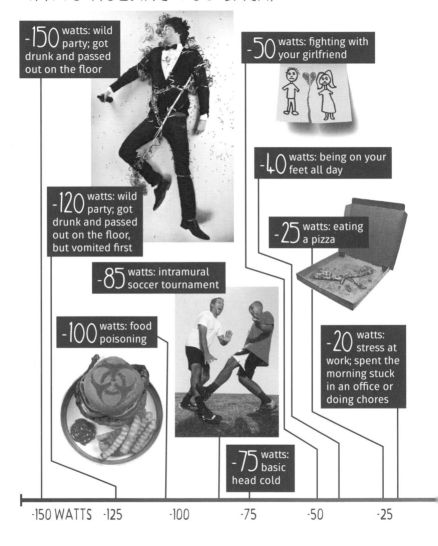

-150 watts: wild party; got drunk and passed out on the floor

-50 watts: fighting with your girlfriend

-40 watts: being on your feet all day

-120 watts: wild party; got drunk and passed out on the floor, but vomited first

-25 watts: eating a pizza

-85 watts: intramural soccer tournament

-100 watts: food poisoning

-20 watts: stress at work; spent the morning stuck in an office or doing chores

-75 watts: basic head cold

-150 WATTS -125   -100   -75   -50   -25

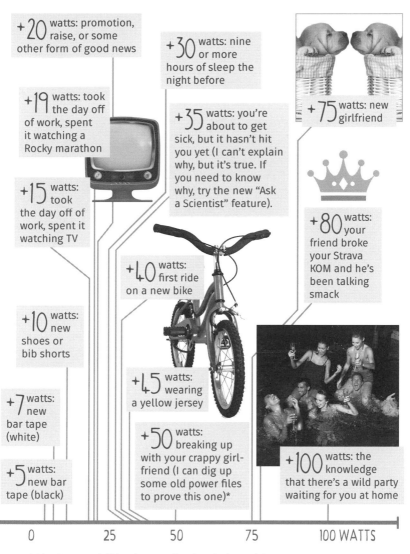

+20 watts: promotion, raise, or some other form of good news

+30 watts: nine or more hours of sleep the night before

+19 watts: took the day off of work, spent it watching a Rocky marathon

+35 watts: you're about to get sick, but it hasn't hit you yet (I can't explain why, but it's true. If you need to know why, try the new "Ask a Scientist" feature).

+75 watts: new girlfriend

+15 watts: took the day off of work, spent it watching TV

+80 watts: your friend broke your Strava KOM and he's been talking smack

+40 watts: first ride on a new bike

+10 watts: new shoes or bib shorts

+45 watts: wearing a yellow jersey

+7 watts: new bar tape (white)

+50 watts: breaking up with your crappy girlfriend (I can dig up some old power files to prove this one)*

+100 watts: the knowledge that there's a wild party waiting for you at home

+5 watts: new bar tape (black)

0   25   50   75   100 WATTS

* I had an ex-girlfriend get really pissed about this.

Q **Do you watch the Tour de France or bike racing at all on TV? Do you see things that regular spectators don't?**

I have mixed feelings when I watch bike racing. Usually, I'm frustrated because I'd rather be in the race than watching it, but my love of the sport usually overcomes that. I don't think I see anything differently than you would (other than the fact that I'm partially colorblind),* but there are certain things I tend to watch for. For example, when a team rides the front for a day when they don't have any obvious reason to, I wonder if they're just trying to get their sponsors on TV, or if another team might be writing them a check.† I also like how announcers try to build suspense by pretending that the early breakaway has a chance, when we all know what's going to happen.

My favorite is when reporters don't get what's going on, like when SportsCenter tried to cover the Tour de France when Lance was winning. "Armstrong is still leading the race, but he finished 136th on the stage? Whatever." They once showed an overhead view of him riding off to the side

---

* I have a sofa that I swear is green, but everyone insists it is blue. The same thing happened with a friend's car. I'm still convinced that this is a bizarre, elaborate hoax.

† I know guys who've gotten $1,000 a day to ride the front for another team.

of the pack: "Here's the leader, staying out of trouble." He was clearly relieving himself.

Q **You've mentioned that you like group rides for training. Since you've probably done them all over the country, what are some similarities and differences?**

I do love a good group ride. It's almost as much fun as a race, minus the need to save energy, so you can really go nuts, but it's not mentally taxing like an interval. The biggest similarity is the people. It seems like every group ride has a common cast of characters. Some of these overlap, but see if you can match most or all of them to folks on the ride you do at home. Maybe we could play Bingo somehow.

The Cocky Pro: I'll start with myself on this one (no one is safe here!). I'll show up and make sure you know I've been riding for four hours already, but I'm still going to drop you if it goes uphill, and even though I'm a climbing specialist, I'll win the sprints. This is my job. I'll go back to my crappy house in my crappy car,* and I'll be on the road most of the year getting my teeth kicked in by the cocky pros from other

---

* I have since traded the Toyota for a Lexus Hybrid, but it was used.

towns, so you won't have to deal with me very often. Let me have this victory.

The Time Nazi: If the ride officially starts at 8 a.m., he's clipping in and rolling off, even if you're still sipping your coffee.

The Superfan: He wears the complete kit (sometimes including the bike) of his favorite team. If it weren't for the gut and the hairy legs, you'd swear it was George Hincapie. He signed up for the special Eurosport package from his cable company, and he will ruin the ending if you DVRed the Tour stage.

Inexplicably Strong Big Guy: You can't figure it out, but no matter how hard the climb is, he's right there every time you look back. The guy doesn't race, his helmet is crooked, and you know you're much stronger than he is, but he keeps coming back, like the Freddy Krueger of cycling.

Shortcut Guy: He joins in somewhere in the middle of the ride, when everyone else is already a little tired. He goes to the front and uses his fresh legs to make you suffer, but when the sprint approaches, he's disappeared like a ghost.

Guy Who Waits for No One: He cruises through the yellow light, even though it's clear that the whole group won't make it, and keeps on motoring. If you complain, he'll say you should ride at the front if you don't want to miss the break. He hopes you'll get a flat so he can leave you stranded.

Team Tactics Guy: Yes, it's a team sport, but there's no prize money, so you shouldn't "block" on the group ride just because you have a teammate up the road. This is exercise. God, you're annoying.

Mountain Biker: "I just do this road stuff for training, bro," he explains, as he finds crazy lines through the corners, bunny-hops curbs, and shows off his skills by taking pointless risks on descents.

Bike Nerd: He has all the newest stuff before it's even available to the public. You've only seen photos of it on Mark Cavendish's bike, but he's got it. He says he knows a guy, just so you understand he doesn't pay retail. Bike Nerd has a ton of bikes and spare parts out the wazoo (he even has a spare wazoo), but you heard he lives in a trailer.

Aerobars Guy: No matter how many times you yell at him, he's going to be in the aerobars in the middle of the group. He'll even take corners in them, and you'll cringe as you watch him barely keep his bike upright, secretly hoping he doesn't.

The Rustbucket: He rides an old steel frame, with downtube shifters, threads sticking out of his tires, and clipless sandals. He can't hold a straight line. If he sneezes, his whole rig will turn to dust.

The Geezer: He's been showing up on this ride since it was all penny-farthings. He might die after an intermediate sprint, and they'll have to peel his rotting flesh off his Selle Italia or just bury him right there.

You might have noticed that I didn't mention any women here. It's not because I'm sexist, it's because of . . .

The Creep: If a woman shows up on the ride, he's all over it. She just wants a workout like the rest of us, but The Creep is full of unsolicited advice, pushes her up the hills as an

Group ride. See if you can spot The Creep.

excuse to touch her butt, and offers her a free bike fit at his house. She won't come back.*

Q What do you think of Lance Armstrong?

Whoa! Shhhhhh! Haven't you heard of omertà? I can't talk about that! Crap, I've already said too much. Delete! Delete!

---

* This mention of The Creep scaring away the women was the punchline of the whole thing, but I still got hate mail for not mentioning enough female riders.

Q Anti-doping wants to know where you are and what you're doing at all times. What's the process, how much really has to be documented, and how do you feel about it?

As you might suspect, it's pretty complicated, and the doping agencies have different levels of scrutiny for different people. You're referring to out-of-competition testing, which is a pretty small pool. USADA can show up at anyone's door (okay, maybe not Obama's, but almost anyone's), but you don't have to actually report your whereabouts unless you're chosen for the out-of-competition testing pool. I don't know exactly what it takes to be selected for that, but I only had it for a year and a half out of my four years as a pro. Maybe they don't think I'm very good now, or perhaps they trust me? So, to address that part of your question, USADA doesn't care where I am or what I'm doing these days.*

The testing process itself is very official and buttoned-down. I think in most cases they outsource local nurses (or

---

* Those were good times, but I have to report whereabouts now. Have you ever gone home with a woman and had to ask for her address to tell the authorities? Me neither, because they never take me up on the offer for a free bike fit, even though I generously gave them a push up the hill.

sex offenders) to do the testing.* Once the tester enters your house, you can't leave their sight. As you chug water, hoping you'll be able to go soon, they read all the forms out loud and explain the whole process, which is infuriating because you've heard it all before and just want to sign and get it over with. Once you've inspected the A and B bottles and matched the numbers to the forms and the package, you go pee, and they have to watch it come out of your body. You go into a plastic cup, just like at the doctor's office, and then you pour it into the A and B bottles, place them into a foam box, like a Mont Blanc pen, and seal everything up.

Once the samples leave your house, I understand they're shipped to France where labels are removed, and cups are tossed randomly into a ball pit like the one at Chuck E. Cheese's, only it's full of urine and bits of broken glass. Or, if you have friends in the right places, they'll throw them out for you. That's just what I hear. Dammit, delete! Delete!

---

* Recently had a guy leave my building by jumping the gate with a bag of my blood, because he didn't want to ask me to buzz it.

Q I'm a recreational rider, but I am considering hiring a coach. I've noticed a number of pro cyclists offer coaching services, but some of them seem to have coaches themselves. Can you explain that? Do most pros have coaches?

Yes, a lot of pros do coaching work on the side.* It's a good way to share their experience and expertise to make a few extra bucks. As far as coaches having coaches, I see how that would seem to hurt their credibility. But it would be worse for a coach to say he doesn't have anything left to learn. Plus, it's hard to be objective about your own fitness and training, even with a power meter. Do doctors prescribe their own medicine? I don't see why not. Pros need the money, and any coach knows enough to help a recreational rider make some improvements. Now, if you find out that your coach's coach has a coach, then you should worry.

Q After a crash, why do pros get up and continue, even if they're going to drop out of the race? Why don't they just get into a car and quit right there?

I can think of several reasons to continue after a crash:

---

* Me, and everyone on my team at the time. We were destitute.

1. You usually don't know right away how badly a crash has hurt you, so it makes sense to test yourself before you give up.

2. In the short term, crashing gives you an adrenaline rush that provides about 30 minutes of invincibility and angry strength, like picking up a star in a Nintendo Mario game. It'll hurt the next morning, but you might as well chase back and attack while the chemicals in your brain allow it.

3. If your job is to race a bike, the least you can do is pretend that you care enough to keep going, especially if you're on TV. This is a hard man's sport, so make a good pain face for the camera. The fans and sponsors appreciate the Johnny Hoogerland* types who limp across the line into a waiting ambulance, and we do get masochistic pleasure out of pushing through it.

---

* Hoogerland was one of the pioneers of being taken out by a race vehicle.

4. There's also a dumb animal aspect to most sports. The harder you're going, the more your actions are based on instinct than careful consideration. All you think about in a race is how to win for your team, and that mind-set doesn't wear off just because you hit the deck. You just see a wheel and know you need to get back to it. We'd probably all follow that lead motorcycle right off a cliff like lemmings if our heart rates were high enough.

Q I've noticed a lot of the riders and teams at the Tour have their hopes dashed with bad luck with crashes early in a stage race. How do you stay motivated in a race when your main goals become unattainable early on?

First of all, how dare you use the word "when" instead of "if" in this context? But I'll give you the benefit of the doubt, because I have found myself—and my team—in that situation. Unfortunately, all you can do is adjust your goals. Once there's no hope of a GC result, we go for stage results. If we have no hope for stage results, we go for the breakaways.

When you run out of goals completely, the race turns into a combination of training, tourism, and entertainment. I've only experienced this once, at the Amgen Tour of California in 2009.

Tour of California 2009.

My team was outmatched and not doped, so I'll admit that we resorted to plain and simple shenanigans. If you can't accomplish anything, you might as well have fun. During the fourth day of freezing, spitting rain, we lined up behind the Astana team and threw full bottles at street signs, so it would make a loud "dong" sound just as the first riders passed. If you timed it right, they'd flinch and look back with a scowl. Some of the other teams even got into it. Tom Boonen had so much fun, he sent one of his teammates back for more bottles.*

Q What was your favorite race and favorite moment of 2012, and why?

That's an easy one. My favorite race was definitely the Redlands Bicycle Classic this year, because I won it. It's easily the most prestigious and most difficult race in the history of athletic competition.

The best moment was at training camp in Tucson, when the team had a professor from Arizona State University lecture us on social media and sponsor representation.

---

* There's nothing better than the middle third of a flat sprint stage.

Professor: "Things like politics, religion, anything divisive like that, you should go ahead and avoid entirely. You'll only alienate people."

Shawn Milne: "What about doping? Can we comment on that?"

Professor: "No, I'd avoid that, too."

Frankie Andreu: "Well, wait a minute. What if they want to comment on a recent story or discuss doping's effect on cycling?"

Me: "Just let your wife do it for you."

A lot of the guys were new, and still intimidated by Frankie,* so the room went silent until he laughed.

---

* I was so proud of this obnoxious joke, I found a way to put it in a magazine.

PART 2
CONTINENTAL PRO

I discovered that the snowy winter in Maryland was a bad trade-off given my skinniness. I thought about pounding cookies and cheeseburgers until I was warmer, but I fled south to Georgia instead. My 2012 season was good enough to earn a spot on the BISSELL Pro Cycling Team* in 2013, on an actual salary,

---

* They asked me to capitalize BISSELL to distinguish the company from the name Bissell, since it's owned by actual people. Mark Bissell is a cool dude. He might even read this. Hi, Mark!

and my business was going pretty well. So I bought a house in Athens, Georgia, with furniture and everything, and had a bunch of friends and teammates move in to help defray the cost. Life was good, and for a couple months, I thought I was on Easy Street. It made me more eager than ever to share advice and help fellow cyclists in my column (as well as in the book I was working on, which eventually became *Pro Cycling on $10 a Day*). Then I decided to shoot for the WorldTour, started training my ass off, and Easy Street dead-ended.

Q How can I get better at criteriums? Should I cut down my long rides? Do more sprints? Hit the gym?

I'm not a huge expert on criterium racing, but you're in luck, because I've spent a lot of time with teammates and close friends Isaac Howe and Luca Damiani over the last few years. They're two of the best crit riders in the country, and I've observed them closely, so I can tell you exactly what Isaac and Luca do that makes them so fast.*

Isaac:

- Stop training, immediately. The less you ride, the better you'll get. If you do have to train, definitely don't work on your sprint, even though it's supposed to be your specialty. Train on climbs and insist that you can make yourself good at them.
- Surround yourself with various stressors to distract yourself from a healthy and productive lifestyle. For

---

* This feels mean now.

example, get some student loans, then buy a car that's falling apart so it will always break down on your way to the race.

- Move into a three-bedroom apartment with five other dudes, because it's okay for grown men to share bedrooms.
- Big biceps are key.
- Never, ever hold in a fart.
- If you break a collarbone and have to fly home to Vermont for treatment, don't worry. Phil won't mind if you leave your car in his driveway all summer.*

Luca:

- Start every third sentence with "In Italy . . ." but pronounce it "Een Eetaly . . ."
- When your pet guinea pig dies, cry inconsolably all night. Mention the deceased rodent several times daily for the rest of your life.
- For breakfast, make green tea in a cereal bowl, add granola or oats, and then cover with honey.

---

* Isaac has gotten his shit together since then, mostly. He still likes criteriums, but he doesn't bother with mountains anymore, and his girlfriend is the only one who has to smell his farts.

- For dinner, make pasta and prosciutto.
- On training rides, if Phil goes too hard up the climb, yell "Grupetto, grupetto," until he either slows down or rides out of earshot.
- Wear a kid's Nintendo Luigi watch you got out of a vending machine and call it your heart-rate monitor.*

Q You hardly raced any criteriums last year. Is that because you're a wuss, or you're just no good at them? What do you do when there's a crit in the middle of a stage race?

I actually do enjoy crits (and the prize money that goes with them), and I'm okay at everything except the sprinting part, but lining up at a crit when I have a stage race coming up isn't always a great idea. Crits are a lot of travel for very little training, and of course, you're much more likely to round a corner into a huge pile of carbon shards and sweaty men, which isn't ideal prep for a stage race.

In a crit that's part of a stage race, GC riders are usually given space at the front, but there's a point near the end

---

* Luca moved back to Italy when Kenda Pro Cycling folded. I never managed to visit him, so our relationship is mostly limited to Instagram, but the love never dies.

when the field sprinters start to take corners four-wide and shoulder-to-shoulder, and I'll slip out of the top 20 to let them do their thing.

You'd hope that my respect would be reciprocated, and that sprinters would get out of my way at the base of a climb, but they never do. When a climb is coming up—even a mountaintop finish—the sprinters always fight for wheels, with the delusion that they can hang on. I can't count how many times someone has tried to knock me off a wheel at the base of a final climb, and I just want to scream: "We know you're not going to be here in 10 minutes. Leave me alone."*

So read this, sprinters: When there's a climb coming up, show me the same consideration I show you in a field sprint.†

Perhaps this does make me a wuss, but I'd argue that climbers are just a more delicate breed of bike racer.

Q **I've always been curious as to how pay works. Do you get a normal check? Does the team cover your travel expenses?**

---

* Have since screamed this many times.

† This didn't work. Sprinters can't read.

Most pro teams handle all the expenses, even for riders who don't get a salary. Once you get to the race, you usually don't open your wallet, and just like a normal job, I get a check in the mail, only it's much smaller. That is, the numbers on it are smaller. The physical check is the standard size. You know what I mean.

Q From the places you've lived, what's your favorite group ride and why?

My favorite rides are the Hipp Ride in Gainesville, Florida, and the WBL series in Athens, Georgia. The Hipp Ride is nice because the roads are empty, and since it's flat, everyone can go just as hard as they want and no one gets dropped if they want to sit on. The WBL series goes on every Saturday in the winter in Athens, Georgia. It's run like a well-oiled machine by a lawyer with a heart of gold.* Local sponsors give discounts on food after the ride, while organization, prizes (for each day and for the overall), neutral support, results, and courses are on par with most local races.†

---

* Shout-out to Dave Crowe!

† There's nothing like winning $200 and a six-pack in January.

Winter Bike League series, Athens, Georgia.

My least favorite rides would be the Cycle Science ride in South Florida, and The Shootout in Tucson, Arizona. The Cycle Science ride is out and back on A1A (your only choice down there), which is so flat it's like you're going downhill all day, and they don't even look before they blast through the lights. I've been so sure that I was going to die on that ride, I got past the "fear" part and made peace with it.

The Shootout could be a great ride. Lots of pros show up, the roads are empty, and there's a perfect mix of climbing and flats, but it starts at sunrise in Arizona in the winter, and if I were the type that could get up at 5:30 a.m., I'd have a real job. You have to wear tons of layers and ride in the dark to make it to the start. Then when it heats up, you have 90 pounds of sweaty clothes to drag up the climbs.

Q **Do you take any supplements? Are you afraid to test positive from tainted products? Have you ever had any issues with that?**

I do take some supplements, but you have to be careful. There are a few different certifications and independent tests that manufacturers go through to prove that their products are clean, so I look for them first, and I mostly take basic, natural antioxidants or simple vitamins. If the bottle has a sweaty dude with huge muscles on it, I stay away. If it has a sweaty, athletic woman on it, I might stare for a minute, but I won't buy it. If there's a jar of DHEA from the same brand in the next aisle, that's a deal-breaker.

The only issue I've ever had with supplements was a multivitamin that's not on the market anymore. It was aimed at endurance athletes, completely clean, but included something like 14,000 percent of the recommended daily value of vitamin B6 and B12.* Those aren't toxic in a megadose, but your body has to filter it out, and

---

* Yeah, 13,900 percent is enough.

a few years of that can do damage to your bladder lining. I had to pee constantly for a while until I stopped taking it, and I only figured it out after I saw a proctologist, and you know what that means. The moral of the story is that taking supplements can be fine if you do it right, but if you screw up, you could get suspended from racing (or worse: You have to see a proctologist).

Q How does it work when teams have riders from different countries? Does language factor into a team's decision on who to hire? Are there ever any culture clashes?

Language is definitely a factor in hiring decisions. Most teams have a dominant language, based on the nationality of their sponsors and management, and guys from other countries have to learn if they want to join. On Kenda, we only had a few foreign riders. Luca Damiani is Italian, but his English is solid. One year we had Ben Day on the team from New Zealand (just kidding, Ben! I know you're from Australia*). I'm not sure what language they speak there,

---

* Everywhere I've been has another place nearby that they look down on. In Georgia, they make fun of Alabama. Australians are like that with New Zealand. Someone, please let me know who they make fun of in Syria. Also, I love the assumption that Ben Day was reading my column.

but that was a tough language barrier to overcome (dead serious about that part, Ben. I never understood a word you said).

Some of my new teammates on BISSELL actually are from New Zealand. All I know about people from New Zealand is that you're not supposed to call them filthy kiwis. (I learned that when my foreign-exchange math teacher in 10th grade sent me to the principal's office.)

One year, my director hired a Somali pirate as a guest rider. His English was good, but he kept taking hostages in the team car.

As far as culture clashes, Luca and I had a long-running war about bathroom etiquette. I'm a firm believer in "when it's yellow, let it mellow, but when it's brown, flush it down." But his policy is "when you roommate with me, you flush everything." I think that sort of waste might explain why the Italian economy is in trouble, but we get the same sort of clashes between American riders. I went to college in Florida, and we didn't know how to respond when a teammate from California told everyone to "Stop rifling my chill!" Forcing a bunch of random, awkward introverts to socialize and get along is part of what makes this sport so beautiful.

Q What are the travel logistics like for a pro?

I once sat next to a soigneur on an airplane. She was studying a bunch of arrival times and addresses in a little book.

"What are you doing?" I asked.

"You think this just happens magically, don't you?" she said. "You think it's just a coincidence that someone picks you up 20 minutes after you land and everything is taken care of."

I'm not sure what she was talking about. Of course it's magic.

Athletes are generally treated like big, dumb animals, so I'm happy to report that I have no idea how the logistics work for travel. I get an e-mail with my flight information, I pack a suitcase, and I get on the plane. When I land, I wander over to baggage claim, pick out my suitcase (or at least one that looks similar), and stand around in the pickup area. Without fail, someone in a car marked BISSELL shows up and tells me to get in. They take me to a hotel, where my bike is built and tires are pumped, and someone else hands me a room key. The next day, they point me in a direction and instruct me to pedal.

Q Where was the worst place you had to race your bike, and why?

I've have so many horrible memories from horrible places I've raced, this question is like if you asked a parent which child is their favorite. I've done nighttime criteriums in urban areas where the only safe way to warm up was laps around a parking garage, and I've raced through parts of Alabama where locals pelted the pack with cigarettes and beer cans, but the Tour of the Demilitarized Zone in Korea takes the cake. The Tour de DMZ was such a bad idea, you'd think I made it up. We raced for three days, right along the barbed wire between North and South Korea. The only spectators were soldiers with M16s, and we all choked on dust kicked up from low-flying military helicopters.

Q When going into a race, what homework do you do to give yourself the best chance of a successful outcome?

I like to drive the time trial course if I've never done it before, and I'll look at the technical guide to memorize where the time bonuses, KOMs, and feed zones will be. Most of the races I plan to do this year I've done once or twice before, so I know what's coming up.

For bigger events, like California or Colorado, I might get a chance to pre-ride a climb if I'm lucky, but usually, we all just wing it. Guys in my line of work are those who had problems with homework.*

Leading up to the race, we look over all the stages to come up with a general strategy, and in the daily pre-stage meeting, we brush up on the plan for the day. That's about the most you'll get out of us. We're lucky that bike racing isn't very complicated.

Q **I've noticed that when I wear my team kit, local Cat. II racers wave at me, but when I wear something mismatched, they stare straight ahead. Why is that?**

I hope this isn't politically incorrect or offensive, but riders who wear matching kits are superior to those who don't. If I'm wearing my full kit with matching helmet and bike, but my base layer doesn't match, I'm ashamed to be seen in public. If they're looking pro and you're not, they're right to snub you, and you shouldn't ever expect a pro to look you in the eye as if you are equals. In fact, you have no right to be enjoying this fine publication. Put the magazine down.

---

* And authority. And being inside.

We don't like your kind around here. [The opinions of Phil Gaimon do not necessarily reflect those of *VeloNews*. Direct your hate mail to @philgaimon on Twitter. —Ed.]

Q Are you excited about your new Pinarello Dogma? Are there any bikes you get attached to? Do you give them names?

Of course I'm excited! Pros are just bike nerds at heart, or at least we all started out that way.* New Bike Day is a highly anticipated, almost religious holiday for us. I think it goes New Bike Day, Christmas, New Kit Day, then Cyclists's Birthday (all cyclists celebrate their birthdays on January 1, when our racing age goes up).

I try not to get too attached to any bikes, though. You have to hate it to thrash it properly, and I take pride in putting my bike through lots of long days in the elements. The biggest reason, though, is that I know I'll be getting a new one every year, or I could snap it in half piling into the Cat. II who wouldn't wave at you, and I don't want to feel like I've lost a loved one. It's the same reason why soldiers didn't make friends in foxholes.

---

* I used to go to bike shops just to look. Like a museum.

Q How can I avoid flat tires?

Stop riding bikes.

Q Is cycling still fun when it's a job?

When I first turned pro, I was worried that I wouldn't enjoy riding so much. The word "amateur" comes from "amo," Latin for "love," implying that amateurs do it for the joy, and professionals don't. I'm happy to report that the Romans got it wrong. Riding a bike professionally is more fun in my opinion, because I feel like I got something over on society. Those Romans were always a little bit off, anyway. That's probably why they built those "ruins" all over Europe.

Q What's it like to wake up in the hospital after crashing on your face?

For readers who don't follow the U.S. racing scene, this question is either an amazing coincidence or a reference to the San Dimas Stage Race in March 2013 where I was leading the GC after winning the opening time trial, but my handlebar clipped a fence, sending me over the bars and onto my face. I was unconscious for several minutes, so they

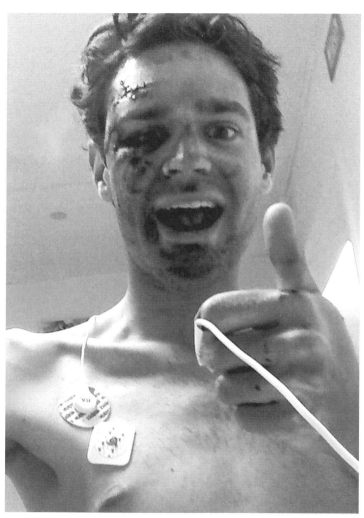

Face crash, San Dimas 2013.

airlifted me to the county hospital in Los Angeles, where all the illegal aliens, gang members, bike racers, and drug addicts end up.

I don't remember crashing, but I'm still 100 percent sure it wasn't my fault, because I don't make mistakes (I bite the erasers off all my pencils). I've heard a rumor that when I was passed out on the course, I peed my shorts, but I'm 75 percent sure that someone made it up.

I vaguely recall the helicopter ride, but my first clear memory was speaking to a nurse, trying to piece together what happened.* I knew I was in a bike race, but I couldn't remember where. When I tried to move my head to examine my surroundings, my neck muscles protested with pain, refusing to lift my sore noggin from the pillow after all they'd been through. I figured the neck was broken, so I grabbed a handful of hair with my left hand, and lifted my head manually.

They must have cut off my clothing, because I could see half a pair of BISSELL shorts in a paper bag in the corner (no, I couldn't tell whether or not they were urine-soaked from that distance).

---

* Also tried to get her number, with my face torn up. Unsuccessful.

"Nurse, did you cut a jersey off, too?"

"Yes, we did," she confirmed.

"Do you remember what color it was?" I had a hunch that I might have been doing well in the race before the crash.

She looked in the paper bag. "It's yellow," she said, removing the bloody, torn, race leader's jersey.

"I'm going to need more morphine, please." She must have wondered why I hated yellow so much.

I was kicked out of my bed for a meth addict who'd been stabbed but wouldn't share his name with the police, and I couldn't hear much after that, over all the shouting. Since VeloNews.com had reported that I was airlifted from the race, when BISSELL's director, Omer Kem, arrived with my bag and phone, I had hundreds of texts, e-mails, and voice-mails from concerned friends, family, and strangers. I spent an hour trying to respond to everyone, but it was exhausting, and I already had a headache. My morphine-saturated brain thought it would save time to tweet a shirtless photo of myself, giving the thumbs-up and grinning through a black eye, to tell the world how well I was doing.

Maybe I should leave the erasers on my pencils after all.*

---

* The "delete" key is downright worn-out.

Q **Do you ride at a specific time, or just when you feel like it?**

I only ride when I feel like it, which just happens to be at 10:30 every morning.

Q **Do you have a special diet? It seems like a lot of pros are gluten-free. What effect does that have on performance?**

I don't have any major allergies, so I look at diet with the combined goals of performance and not being annoying at a restaurant. Science says that reducing dairy and gluten will make you go faster and recover better, so I avoid those as best I can, without calling myself anything-free. I have noticed that I barely fart anymore, but it's hard to say how that translates to the bike.* If you're not having any digestion problems and you're not a professional chasing marginal gains, I'd try not to overthink your diet. Horses eat nothing but hay, and they're still ripped and fast.†

---

* I've always had this dream where I'm in a two-up sprint with someone, and just as I'm throwing my bike, I fart, and the propulsion makes the difference.

† I got hate mail from a horse person about this. They eat other things, too. Whatever.

Q I've been training a lot and noticing plenty of improvement on the bike, but I don't feel like I'm much more fit in general. Do you find that your high VO_2max and lactate threshold translate to more practical areas in life?

The only time my VO_2max came in handy off the bike was when I forgot the pump for my air mattress. It was a queen size, and I got it nice and firm with pure lung power, but if you have a better memory for that sort of thing, you might not notice much. Cycling is a very specific exercise. If you're already fit, bikes will improve your ability to pedal in circles, but you're probably just as likely to be out of breath at the top of the stairs. And forget about opening jars or being more attractive with your shirt off.*

Q How do you get embrocation off your legs?

The best way to handle embro is to live somewhere warm, because nobody ever has trouble removing sunscreen. I've had an unfortunate number of snowy rides this year, though, so I now have plenty of embro experience. The first time I tried to remove it, I experienced the infamous burning

---

* I have a four-and-a-half pack.

sensation and eventually resorted to the "beating my head with a stick" method. I don't remember if that worked or not. I hear that rubbing alcohol works, but BISSELL is sponsored by Chamois Butt'r,* so they send me plenty of free SkinWash, which does the job well. So your options are:

1. Win a few races and get a pro contract,

2. Buy stuff at the bike shop like an amateur, or

3. Find a big enough stick to distract you from the pain.

Q I've noticed guys taking a "nature break" while they're riding in a race. Is there a certain zone for that, like a feed zone? Is it planned in advance? Is this unique to European racing?

Rolling "nature breaks" aren't planned, partly because there won't suddenly be a day when men no longer have to urinate randomly. Do you write "exhale" in your schedule, or do you just breathe out sometime after you breathe in? There's no specified zone for it, either, because imagine

---

* Chamois Butt'r was always very nice to me.

that for spectators! It would be like the front row at Sea-World ("You will get wet!"), only with urine.* It's understood that the race slows down when the early break goes, and that's the time and place to pee (as long as you're not in the breakaway).

The rolling pee is less common in the U.S., because our races are a little shorter, a lot less organized tactically, and I guess I'll admit that the European guys are just better at everything, bodily functions included. I heard a story about one guy (who shall remain nameless . . . Mancebo), who pooped into a musette bag at the back of the field during a race. What a pro!

I practice the rolling nature break during almost every race, and I'm dismayed at guys who call themselves pros but can't do it. It's something you have to work on in training, but it's an important skill for any bike racer. In fact, I think it should be a requirement to get your Category I upgrade from USA Cycling. "I'm sorry, your request for an upgrade has been denied. You have more than enough upgrade points, and your race results are impressive, but that stream was weak, and it got all over your shoe."

---

* I've seen that porno.

Q **I heard that there was an old Euro tradition against shaving your legs the night before a race, because it saps energy. Is this true? Does anyone follow that?**

I don't know what leg-shaving technique they use in Europe, but I've never found leg shaving to tire me out. Perhaps Europeans shave more vigorously than I do.*

Q **In my races, we often see average speeds of close to 30 mph, but in training, I average 17 to 18 mph. What would a pro rider's average speed be for a 100-mile solo ride? Also, how long does this take them?**

Average speed depends on terrain, obviously. In Florida, it wasn't uncommon to average 24 mph for a long ride, or to go several hours without shifting. I'd say a rough average in training rides these days would be 20 mph.

For the second part, is this an "Ask a Pro" question or a fifth-grade math problem? I'm not sure how long it would take to do 100 miles at 20 mph (if I had my calculator, I could totally do it, though). I think that might be almost four hours. For Euro pros, add another 90 minutes

---

* Euro pros have all sorts of dumb superstitions, like air conditioning gets you sick because it circulates germs from other rooms, and plants in your hotel room absorb oxygen and hurt recovery.

for coffee stops and hourly breaks to apply cologne and hair gel.

Q **I saw you almost won the U.S. national road championship in Chattanooga, but you were caught by the group near the end and finished with nothing, so I'm sure you were disappointed. What's the correct way to praise a cyclist on a good performance, even if they might not be happy about it?**

Indeed, my inbox was flooded after the national championships with congratulations for something I regarded as a failure. I appreciated the kind words, but it was hard to take. You wouldn't high-five an airline pilot for almost hitting the runway.*

"Nice effort, Phil!" might have been appropriate, but if an athlete is truly unhappy with a result, I think the healthiest way to handle it is to look ahead to the next goal, rather than dwell on the negative. So, thanks for bringing it up! In general, try to take into account the rider's expectations. If he collapsed into a crying heap after the finish, pounded his handlebars in frustration, or cursed at the media, he probably doesn't want to be congratulated.

---

* Sully landed in the Hudson River after this, just to prove me wrong.

Q I've been racing for a long time, hoping to make it someday as a pro, but between weather, crashes, and long stages, it just looks like the higher up you get, the more brutal the lifestyle. Is being a pro cyclist everything it's cracked up to be?

Like anything in life, pro cycling is a little less glamorous the deeper you get into it, just as the magic trick isn't as impressive to the rabbit crammed inside the hat. Tough as it is, though, bike racing is still awesome. After all the bruises, cramps, and long days, the hardest part is keeping a straight face when I get my paycheck.*

Q What does a team do when a rider is sick or injured? Does he still get paid?

They usually just shoot him and send him to the glue factory. He's of no use to the sport or society if he can't compete, after all. Oh wait, you said rider, not racehorse. Of course he still gets paid! Teams understand that sickness and injury happen. In the event of something serious or chronic, general practice is that the rider is offered his

---

* I have a new philosophy now, where I don't get paid for the good days. I've decided that I work those days for free, so I can get paid 10 times as much when I have to ride in the rain, for example.

spot on the team the following year at the same salary, so he keeps his job as long as he's taking the proper steps to recover. No animals or bike racers were harmed in the answering of this question.

Q **I started racing a couple of years ago, and I've been hanging my bib numbers on the wall, but one of my teammates told me that this wasn't "pro." True or false? Do you keep any souvenirs from racing?**

I don't know of any pros who keep their race numbers. By the time you've done enough races to be a pro, you'd need to win the Tour de France to afford a house with enough wall space. Besides, do safety pins penetrate drywall?

For a souvenir, I keep one of each jersey I've worn (team jerseys and awarded ones),* but I wish I'd started saving and labeling hotel room keys when I started. That would have been a cool way to document where bike racing has taken me. But every time I start, I end up with a pocket full of key cards halfway through a stage race, pulling my hair out in the hallway because I forget which one is which.

---

* I threw away two years of Kenda Pro Cycling jerseys, but the memories still haunt me.

I hate to break it to you, but scars are probably the best souvenirs, and since they've been carved and seared into your flesh, you don't have trouble keeping track of them. Maybe get little tattoos with the date and locations of each incident?

Q What advice do you have for a 15-year-old just getting into serious training?

I didn't start racing until I was 19. At 15, I was still burping the alphabet and picking my . . . actually, I just picked my nose a minute ago. I'm the wrong person to ask about the junior scene, but I'll do my best.

I've heard good things about USA Cycling junior camps, and I'm sure it would be helpful to find a coach who knows how to get kids ready for racing without burning them out. The best advice I can give is something my grandfather told me a long time ago: "If you have to pick your nose, make sure that no one is looking."

Q We've all seen dogs run into the peloton in a race, but I was recently caught up in a midrace crash caused by a deer. What's the scariest beast that you've ever encountered while racing, and how did you deal with it?

The scariest beast I can think of is the newly upgraded Cat. II at his first big race. When pro teams show up, and the local boy is racing the big event he's always dreamed of, he'll forget that pavement hurts and will bomb every corner like there's no stage 2. Even off the bike, he shows no mercy, wearing calf compression socks in public. Women see this beast in his natural habitat (a Subway or a Starbucks) and assume that all bike racers are ridiculous, bringing more shame to a sport with enough problems already.

I deal with it in the same way that pros dealt with me when I first got my Cat. II license (I didn't have a compression-wear sponsor back then, but I certainly fell down a few times for no reason). On the bike, I yell and cuss liberally, but not because I'm a jerk. It's a tactic for my safety—nothing personal—and they'll understand someday.* Off the bike, I wear dark sunglasses to avoid eye contact with the Cat. II beast. If women suspect that I'm a geeky bike creature, I insist that no, I'm a vacuum salesman.

---

* "You'll understand why I'm condescending to young people when you're older."

Q Now that you'll be riding for Garmin-Sharp in 2014, do you know what your schedule will be next year?

I haven't nailed it down with Jonathan Vaughters, the team director, exactly, but I figure I'll hit the gym pretty hard in the off-season to bulk up for Flanders and Paris-Roubaix. I'm not sure if I'll be team leader on the cobbles, exactly, but someone has to chase down Fabian for the sprinters. After that, I'll ride up a few mountains for training, and I expect I'll do the Giro d'Italia, as preparation for the Tour de France. And after I win the Tour, I'll cash in on those post-Tour criteriums, put on 20 pounds, buy a Ferrari or two, and maybe come back for world's, if I feel like it.

Q I've never tried racing, but I love riding my bike, so I'm thinking about quitting my job to see if I can make it as a pro cyclist. What steps would you recommend to get started?

Really? Because I've never thrown a spiral, but I love the smell of sweaty men and fresh-cut grass, so I'm thinking about quitting cycling to become a quarterback in the NFL. Or does that make me sound clueless and delusional?

Q How do you feel about how bad Brad Wiggins sucked in 2013?

I wouldn't say he sucked, exactly, but it's hard to understand why he didn't come closer to our expectations. My guess is that Wiggins made a lot of sacrifices* to accomplish what he did in 2012, and with all those yellow jerseys and a gold medal on the wall, it was probably tough to put himself through it again. Once you perfect something, you've outgrown it in a way. Wouldn't you get bored doing the same puzzle over and over? Now imagine if one of the requirements to finish the puzzle was not eating a piece of cake for a year and doing countless hill repeats in the rain. Finally, pretend you're already a millionaire and a knight, so you don't have to do anything that you don't want to. Maybe losers like us can never really understand.[†]

Q According to Twitter, you train with a giant saddlebag. Is this true? How can you do something that's so un-pro?

---

* Sacrifices and . . . compromises.

[†] I bought a sword, so I'm close enough to a knight that I'm not a loser anymore.

I notice a lot of guys who are too cool for a saddlebag, and I wonder how they can get away with it. The answer, of course, is that they don't train all that much. It is shameful to carry a suitcase up all the hills, but you know what's more shameful? Walking home.*

---

* Big saddlebag, and keep that Di2 charged, kiddos. That's the "pro cyclist's walk of shame."

PART 3
WORLDTOUR PRO

I drove west to train with Tom Danielson
in Tucson, and then was sucked further
west when a friend offered to let me stay
at his house in Big Bear for free, because
altitude training was all the rage then
(and free housing is, was, and will always
be all the rage). When the 2013 season
was over, I was supposed to head back
to Georgia, but I met a girl and moved to
Los Angeles. Then we split up, but I liked
all the palm trees, so I kept LA as my base

when I wasn't off racing in Europe. Part 3 covers two years on Slipstream (Garmin-Sharp in 2014 and Cannondale-Drapac in 2016), with a year on Optum in between.

Q When you are on the road for extended periods of time, how do you keep a normal routine?

One summer when I was an amateur, I kept a routine that would have impressed a German train conductor.* I made oatmeal and eggs for breakfast every morning and jumped on my bike at exactly 10:30 a.m., exchanging a smile and wave with an old man coming the other way. He must have had an equally strict schedule, since we'd always pass each other at the same spot. One day, he ran into me a block earlier than usual, so he shook his head with a "tsk, tsk" gesture, chastising me for leaving late. I didn't let the geezer down again.

Back then, though, I wasn't racing a whole lot. These days, I don't have enough time at home to even establish a normal routine. I try to go to bed around the same time every day, but other than that, I just embrace the madness. Since races all start at different times, and we jump between time zones

---

* A Jamaican train conductor would have said I should chill out, a French one would be on strike, an American one would say I should get a car. A Canadian one would just say "sorry," and . . . I'll stop.

so much, being regimented like the old man would only cause more stress. The best you can do to stay comfortable on the road is to take it one day at a time and stay flexible. To avoid homesickness, I keep in touch with friends, and I travel with my own soap and shampoo, so at least I don't have to put up with the cheap hotel stuff.*

Q Can you take your bike apart and put it back together?

Taking a bike apart is no feat. Any idiot with opposable thumbs and a set of Allen keys could get pretty far and easily finish the job with an axe. The same goes with a space shuttle, I imagine. Putting it back together is the tricky part, but I raced as an amateur long enough that I could manage anything outside of the spokes/nipples,[†] and whatever scary bearings explode out of the bottom bracket and the hubs. I think most bike racers are about the same.

Things have changed now that I'm an awesome Euro-pro, because we have mechanics to work on bikes for us.

---

* As of October 2016, I've gone almost two years without soap. Shampoo once a month. Just cold water. You don't need that crap.

† Pretty much made up this question because I wanted to use "nipples" in a column.

The moment I signed a contract with Garmin-Sharp, a little corner of my brain died and I lost all ability to clean or fix my bike. The other day, I tried to change the bar tape and wash the mud off my Cervélo, and I nearly died. Friends found me wrapped up with the tape like a mummy, half-choked by the chain, and I don't even want to tell you where the seatpost was jammed. Lesson learned. Next time I have something to fix on the bike, I'll handle it like I've seen my new teammates do on TV: I'll chuck it over a guardrail and demand a new one.

Q How important is a good massage for your racing and training?

As an amateur, I remember rolling my eyes at the mention of pros getting massaged at races. My mom gets a massage to relax after working at the office. Why would a big, tough athlete need candles and classical music? Then I turned pro, and the soigneur jammed her fists and elbows deep into my thighs to take out all the knots.* Turns out, there are different kinds of massage. The ones we get hurt like hell, but you definitely feel better the next day.

---

* Alyssa Morahan was the soigneur this refers to. Any time I thought I might be getting injured somewhere, I'd tell her the spot, she'd make it so I could barely walk, and then the next day I was brand-new.

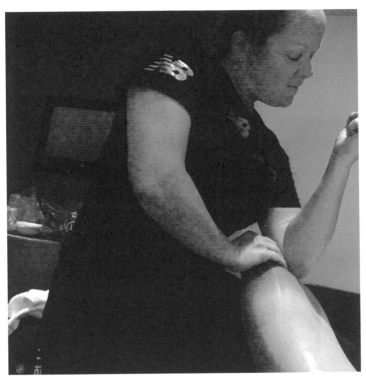
Alyssa, trying to kill me.

Massage is crucial during a stage race. At home, I try to go once a week, but it's only worth it if you find the right kind of massage therapist. Candles and "Songs of the Humpback Whale" won't cut it. Not sure if your therapist is good? Here's how you can tell: If you enjoy it, it's a bad sports massage.

If you find yourself sweating and cringing in pain, that's a keeper. Speaking of which, it's a rule that you can't let them know it hurts or ask them to ease up. You grit your teeth and you take it. You're a big, tough athlete, after all.

Q How do you deal with the ups and downs of being a pro cyclist?

Easy! When I hit an uphill, I push the button on my shifter and it goes to an easier gear. And then at the top of the hill, I hit the other button and the gear gets harder.

If you didn't want the Amelia Bedelia literal answer, that's a little more complicated. Here's a quick summary of life as an athlete: You're training and miserable, you're lonely, you're training and miserable, you're lonely, you win something and everyone loves you for a day, it's over. You learn to even it out a bit, looking ahead or remembering past successes when you're down, trying to savor every minute but keeping your head on straight when you're up. I think the only guy who has really figured it out is Peter Sagan, who just wins every day and keeps riding that way. Until I learn to sprint like Sagan, I'll just have to cope. I'll be able to explain it better when I'm done with this murder spree . . . I mean training ride.

Q What would be a typical interval session for you?

That's a trick question, because there's nothing typical about the mad power I lay down in my intervals. But I'll answer it anyway. When you race as much as we do, you don't have time for a ton of training during the season, and the speed and high-end stuff happens naturally in the pack. At home, I focus on getting the steady endurance back and trying to maintain my lactate threshold for the climbs and time trials, which means plenty of 20-minute intervals. If there's a race coming up with very specific demands, I'll look for intervals that mimic that effort. For example, if I'll be racing up short, rolling hills, I'll do a few sets of 1-minute efforts, with 30 seconds of recovery in between. Either way, the Garmin* head unit typically says "Uncle"[†] on the screen when I'm finished.

Q Now that you're stepping up to the big leagues with Garmin-Sharp, what are you looking forward to in 2014? What are you most afraid of?

---

* Shameless sponsor plug.

† Shameless uncle plug.

One of the many prestigious races I won at office parks in north Florida.

There are a lot of things I'm looking forward to. Unlike smaller American teams, Garmin-Sharp has a bigger budget, more sponsors (meaning lots of cool stuff to play with), and tons of staff to help out with all the details, so I can focus on racing bikes and writing silly columns for *VeloNews*. Mostly, I'm looking forward to racing bigger events. I had a great time the last few years racing in the U.S., but it's weird sometimes. You train so hard, the competition is tough, and it's such a great feeling when you get to post up and celebrate a victory. Then you see a picture of the finish, and the only spectators are a row of garbage cans.

Of course, my fear is failure, the same as everyone else. Winning a race in front of garbage cans would be much better than getting dropped over and over and embarrassing myself on TV,* but I don't expect it to be like that. I've done the training and I've shown I deserve the opportunity, but I won't really know how hard it is or whether I'm ready until I'm in the thick of it and I can feel the ache in my legs. Also, I have a big fear of snakes—because they're icky.

---

* All of the above: Paris-Roubaix 2016.

Q **How do you feel when you see a recreational rider in your Garmin-Sharp kit? Are you offended because they haven't earned it? Should we be afraid to run into you?**

During a training ride recently, I spotted what looked like a teammate at first, with the full kit, POC helmet, and a new Cervélo. Being a team player, my first instinct was to deliver some fresh bottles, but when I got closer, I noticed that he'd put on 50 pounds, was very pale, and his position was rather unorthodox, with an upright stem, very low saddle, and his knees out. I thought, "Maybe Zabriskie really let himself go," but it wasn't him, either. It was just a weekend warrior who'd chosen to buy all our team gear. Maybe I should have done the same seven years ago and saved myself all that trouble.

Was I offended? Do you think LeBron James is offended when he runs into a kid wearing his jersey? Just out of curiosity, if I was, what would you be afraid of? Have you seen my arms? It's probably much safer to offend me than LeBron, but the impostor on the bike path didn't bother me. Quite the contrary: He's a fan, and fans make it possible to do what I do for a living, which I greatly appreciate. I didn't give him those water bottles, though.

Q Would you like fries with that?

Of course I'd like fries with that! Fries are delicious. Sweet potato fries are better.

Q Where can I find the live video feed for the next race you'll be in?

I get this a lot lately. I appreciate your interest, but I honestly don't know which Eurosport network my next UCI 2.1 race will be aired on. I don't even know what time zone I'm headed to. I'm trying to find my passport so I can get there, and researching the safety of the tap water, and whether the power outlets will fry my electric kettle again.* You know, important stuff.

In fact, since I can't possibly watch it myself, live feeds are something I'd never look into. Would you ask Oprah what time her show is on, or would you Google it, perhaps? I can tell you this: It's not going to be on NBC, CBS, ESPN2, or even ESPN237. It will be grainy, there will be offensive pop-up ads, and with 5km to go, when things are really heating up in the race, the feed will freeze and crash your web browser, causing you to pull your hair out in frustration. It'll come back

---

* Went through many kettles, but I gotta have my iced tea.

when they're interviewing the guy who finished second or third. You'll find the results on some form of social media hours later and complain about "spoilers" while I'm shopping online for a new electric kettle.

Q I'm a fan, and I have a collection of pro cycling gear. Can you send me a signed jersey/hat/T-shirt/bottle/kidney/first-born child for my collection?*

We do get a lot of swag, and some of it is given away eventually. Bottles are tossed to souvenir-hunting children after the finish line, and soigneurs are known to give away cycling caps and musette bags in the feed zone. T-shirts are for someone who does the team a favor, like the bus driver at a race. I get a few extra jerseys that go to folks who've let me stay at their house or restaurants that don't charge me for cookies.† You're not likely to get a free jersey from a rider, but if you order one from the team store or just track me down at a race with a marker and bar napkin, I'll gladly sign whatever you want. Please be polite about it, though,

---

* As soon as you join the WorldTour, you're flooded with requests for free things. I had to change my Facebook to a fake name. My life is so hard.

† This list has gotten wonderfully long.

because at some point, you go from "fan" to "guy who's literally demanding the shirt off my back when I'm headed to the bus after a race," and I think that second guy is rude.*

Sending e-mails or messages to random pros has never worked, as far as I know, because now you're asking me to fill out forms at the post office and spend $30 on shipping. I had one note in marginal English, which included a picture of this guy's massive cycling swag collection and candid photos he'd taken of me over the years, which was more likely to earn a restraining order than a free jersey. In all my years, no one has ever offered a trade. I'll contribute to your jersey collection if you contribute to my money collection.

Q Do you take vitamins or supplements? I do, but they make me nervous. Are you afraid they'll be tainted? Do you think they work?

First of all, is there a difference between "vitamin" and "supplement"? I'd be more nervous about losing your friends than testing positive, because you're always wasting their time with redundant questions. Or maybe there is a difference and I'm stupid. I'm not Googling it, because I'm a busy

---

* Belgium.

man (actually, it's because I'm on an airplane, and I'll forget when I land).*

Also, from the department of redundancy department, I've answered this question in a previous column.

Anyway, yes, I do take vitamins and/or supplements. It is scary to wonder whether they're tainted, because getting suspended would be incredibly embarrassing and someone would have to scrape off my CLEAN tattoo. If you do your homework on the different brands, and you don't buy vitamins from dudes in trench coats who stand on street corners, you're probably safe.

It's hard to tell if they work, though. I ate a huge salad yesterday, because salads are good for you, but I don't know if it "worked." Vitamins or supplements might help you recover better and/or get sick a bit less, and those seem like good things.

Q Do you train outside in all weather? How bad does it have to be before it's okay to call off a training ride?

For a few years, I refused to miss a workout, regardless of

---

* I wrote many columns on airplanes. Then I could feel like I earned it if I wanted to buy bottled water at the terminal.

the temperature or precipitation. It made for some miserable days in the snow, and some that were probably downright dangerous, due to the fact that as a cyclist, I have to share the road with large, metal objects, often piloted by incompetents staring at cell phones.

Back then, I thought that training in bad weather made me tough, which was important for some reason. Eventually, you go through enough of those that you're officially tough enough, and riding in conditions that are likely to make you sick or roadkill becomes unwise. I feel that over the course of your life, you only have so many tough days in you, and you should try to budget those for when you need them most. Or maybe I'm just getting soft.

Q I always feel like my legs are ruined after a long drive to a race. How do you handle those miserable flights, transfers, and bus drives?

Wouldn't it be nice if every race were in your backyard? You could just roll out of bed, have some coffee, and go drop all those losers who didn't think to have the race at their house. Of course, the grass on your front yard would be ruined from all the parking, and don't get me started about your bathrooms.

Getting there early is a big help. My team arrives at least a day before a race (three days if you're racing on a different continent), so we have a chance to spin out our legs and settle. If that's not possible, shoot for an hour of riding before the start, just hard enough to get the blood pumping.

In my line of work, almost everyone has to deal with similar travel, so it's usually just a matter of keeping the morale up, which is a challenge when you exit an airport with all your bags, assuming that you've reached your final destination, but then a van picks you up for a three-hour drive (the air conditioning on the van will always be broken in these cases).

Not falling asleep in the back of the van.

One trick I learned from teammate Ben King this year: When you start your travel day, buy a bar of dark chocolate. Every time it occurs to you that you're miserable, break off a row and eat it. So your day still sucks, but at least you have that.

Q On average, how many times per year does a pro cyclist crash?

I haven't seen any survey results, so I can't tell you the exact mean or median, but I can say that in my first year as a pro, I crashed three times. The following year, I crashed twice, but then I put together a solid three-year streak of keeping it upright, which ended with a dramatic whack on the head that nearly killed me in 2013. I would have gladly traded that one for a football field's worth of road rash or 10 broken collarbones.

I think it would be useful to define "crash," though, because that's a tricky word in pro cycling. What if you tumble onto a pile of bodies but never hit the ground? Maybe your bike was broken in half afterward, but you landed on your feet? What if some idiot totally just took your front wheel out and there wasn't anything you could have done?

In my humble opinion, for an incident to be considered a crash, all of the following must happen:

- Your knee, elbow, or hip hits the ground. If you catch yourself with your hand, it counts as a save, just like if you tripped on the stairs. It wasn't graceful, but you made it.

- Some part of your body, clothing, or bike has to be at least slightly damaged. Even if it looked like a full action-movie wipeout, if your helmet was unscathed, your clothes weren't ripped, there's not a scrape on the saddle, your derailleur hanger is still straight, and your bar tape is pristine, that's not a crash.

- Someone has to see you. There was this one time, this guy, let's call him a friend of mine (it wasn't me), hit a patch of ice that just washed his bike out from under me. I mean him. (I've got to get a computer with a backspace key.) But he got up, everything was fine—no bruises, no road rash, and most importantly, no witnesses. Like a tree falling in the forest, that wasn't a crash, either.

Q I want to be as fast as you. What intervals do you do?

That's good thinking. To be fast, all that matters is doing the right intervals. It has nothing to do with base miles, lifestyle, diet, or dedication. In fact, I want to be as handsome as Brad Pitt, so I'm going to ask him what shampoo he uses. I'm sure that'll do the trick. In the meantime, do three sets of 20-minute intervals, and I'm sure we'll be teammates in a year or two.

Q I saw that you're living in Girona, Spain, now. Why do all the Euro pros live there?

It's funny how cyclists end up in clusters. We follow each other around in a big pack all day, so you can't blame us for acting like sheep off the bike as well. In the U.S., they all flock to Boulder, Athens, or Asheville. Europe is similar, with guys in Nice and Lucca, but Girona is definitely the pro cyclist's mecca. It has some nice climbs, beautiful roads in the country and along the coast, and enough friends that there's someone doing the same workout as you every day. It's like Boulder on steroids. I mean, it's like Boulder on EPO. I mean . . . never mind.

Q We see riders praise and thank their teammates after races; they rarely criticize them. I'm sure you've been let down at some point, even if you're not supposed to admit it. What's the worst teammate story you've ever had?

I'm not going to name names, but in the amateur days—or even when I rode as a pro on smaller teams—you don't really have teammates, because if you're not getting paid, there's no incentive to sacrifice yourself for someone else.* Amateurs need results to get onto small pro teams, and workers on those teams probably get $12,000 a year if they're lucky, so they need results to make a living.

I don't criticize them because you can't blame a guy for looking out for himself when he's struggling to pay rent. All you can really do is hope that they consider you an ally and don't race against you for some reason—but even that can be a tall order. Back in the U23 days, we were all racing each other for limited spots on a handful of pro teams, and I was in a breakaway of five riders in the national criterium championships. With five laps to go, I remember looking back and seeing a teammate on the front of the field, right before we got caught. After the race, he said he was just blocking† so we might stay away, but that night we watched the video that his own parents took of the race, and the footage showed otherwise.

"Man, you sure are breathing heavy and shaking your bike a lot for a guy that's blocking," I laughed. "I think I see some drool on your stem."

---

* Aside from "being a nice guy."

† To any amateurs, masters, or guys on the group ride: "Blocking is not a tactic. Knock it off."

His defense: "You'd have finished last out of the five guys in the break, and we wanted better than fifth place."

To be fair, I wasn't much of a teammate that year, either, and he was right, because I'm no sprinter. However, once the breakaway was caught, the guy that chased me was cooked at the finish, and our sprinter was 13th, so maybe 5th would have been pretty good. The sprinter was the only one with a pro contract the next year.*

Q How do you like electronic shifting?

This is a tricky question. Morally, I was always opposed to it. Part of the charm of a bicycle is that it's off the grid: If the apocalypse comes, if we run out of fossil fuels, or the power goes out, the zombies will never catch me on my cable-shifted bike.

Then I tried out the electronic shifting, and I've got to say, it's pretty neat. You push the button, and it changes gears! Shifts are faster and smoother, and moving from the little ring to the big ring goes from "chore" to "downright

---

* I must have still been bitter when I wrote this. I promise I'm over the 2007 U23 Crit championships now. I'm still pissed about the 2013 Pro road race, though.

pleasant." And who doesn't want more "pleasant" worked into their bike rides? For racing and training, I'll happily charge my Di2 once in awhile. But I'll keep one cable-shifted "apocalypse bike" in the basement, just in case. And maybe a chainsaw.

Q What do you eat at stage races? Does the team have a chef?

Garmin-Sharp does have a chef at some of the bigger races, but most of the time, we rely on the race organization and team soigneurs.

In the mornings and evenings, meals are provided by the race—usually buffet-style at the hotel. It's never bad, but just basic food, and it's pretty much the same all around the world. Breakfast is usually standard bread, eggs, and cereal.

After the stage, we rely on soigneurs for lunch and snacks. They prepare postrace sandwiches, and there's always a snack buffet in one of their rooms, with cereal, nuts, fruit, and no chocolate chip cookies whatsoever.

Race dinner is rice, slightly overcooked pasta (with white sauce or red sauce), bread and butter, grilled chicken breast (unseasoned), salad bar, and beef that looks okay, but we're all afraid to eat it because of Alberto Contador.* Most guys travel with their favorite snacks in a suitcase, and in case of an emergency, you can always eat out. As a Continental Pro, I raced a few lower-level stage races fueled by Big Macs, and I did just fine.†

Q What's it like living in Spain with Tom Danielson?

I've had this question a few times, from different types of people. When bike racers ask me, they mean, "What's it like to live with a former doper?" It's like I've infiltrated some evil organization to spy on them and share secrets. Or maybe they think if I opened the wrong cabinet, I'd be buried under an avalanche of 10-year-old syringes and blood bags. I've been through all the cabinets by now, and the only avalanche was a precarious bottle of soy sauce, which made the kitchen smell like a Panda Express for a day.

Others just mean, "What's it like to live with a famous guy?" Well, Tom happens to be one of the best on the planet

---

* Alberto has pet cows, which he adores, and he gets angry if he sees you eating red meat.

† Usain Bolt prefers McNuggets.

at going uphill on a bicycle, but other than that, he's a nor-mal, nice roommate. If I leave a soggy Castelli jersey in the wash, he hangs it to dry for me,* and if Tom runs out of rice milk, he's welcome to mine. Don't touch his almond but-ter, though. That's hard to find here, so Tom flies it in from the U.S.† Come to think of it, I'm not sure where he hides those jars to sneak them past customs, if you get my drift, so maybe I don't want it anyway.

Q **I saw on Jonathan Vaughters's Twitter feed that you rode 4,000 kilometers for training in August last year before your off-season, in a simulated Grand Tour. I'm curious about the timing: Why would you train like that at a time of year when you're not leading up to a race, when you're only going to take a break and lose your fitness?**

After years of racing in the United States, I needed to improve my endurance to step up to the European peloton, but during the season, between 60 or more race days and all the travel and recovery in between, that doesn't leave

---

* He folded it for me once.

† Blendtec sent me a nice blender with what is basically a lawn-mower engine for power. I make my own nut butters now!

much time for training. A fake Grand Tour in December would have ruined my form for the rest of the year, so the fall was the only time it made sense.

It's true that I'd lose most of the fitness in my off-season, but even if you sit on the couch for a year, every pedal stroke makes you a little stronger for the rest of your life, and I think the 2013 Tour de Phil saved me from a few DNFs this season.* Also, and most importantly, Vaughters told me to do it, and I'm not stupid.

Q Post-stage press conferences seem to be filled with whining. Why do pros always have excuses when they don't win? Can't they just say they did their best but they got beaten?

Pros have excuses for the same reason as everyone else: We're paid to get certain results, and sometimes we can't meet those expectations. Imagine that you work at a grocery store, and your giant salsa display topples to the floor. If you tell your boss that you did your best, and there are bits of broken glass everywhere, you're rightfully fired. You have to tell the boss that some dumb kid ran his toy Hot

---

* It did.

Wheels car into it, but you're the best salsa-display builder on the planet, and you'll prove it next time. In fact, you have plans for a full-sized Old El Paso Taj Mahal that will fill the store with art aficionados, who will certainly pick up some impulse buys on their way out.

Just the same, if the team works for a guy and he doesn't win, he has to convince them that he'll do better in the future, or he's out of a job. The next time I find myself in the grupetto, I'll tell the director that I certainly would have won, but some dumb kid ran his Hot Wheels into the bunch.

Q I just bought a new Garmin Edge 510. How do pros set up their Garmins? Do you have pages set up for training and activity profiles for each type of race?

I don't worry about different activity profiles. Like most of the guys on Garmin-Sharp, I just keep an Edge 1000 on my Cervélo R5 training bike at home, an 810 on my Cervélo S3 for flat races, a 510 on my P5 (the sleek look is probably more aero, right?), and the 500 on my other Cervélo R5 for hilly races (it's a little lighter, after all). Then I keep a few spare Garmin 1000s around the house. They're great for doorstops, paperweights, and holding the tarp down over the pool.* We got a lot of free Garmins. No, you can't have one.

Hypothetically, if you were some kind of weirdo who only had one Garmin or one Cervélo, I would set up a training profile, a race profile, and maybe a time trial profile. In training, your main page should have time, power, distance, cadence, and all the other stuff you want to keep an eye on as you go. Your next training page would have your averages, maximums, altitude gain, sunset time if you ride after work, and other numbers you'll want to check once in a while during a workout. I like to make routes beforehand, so I added power and ride time to the map screen, which lets me keep an eye on the workout while I navigate.†

For races and time trials, just keep the minimum info that you need on one screen, because flipping screens while racing would probably void the warranty when you crash. My road race screen just shows power, speed, time, and distance. I haven't set up the training pages on the Garmin

---

* I've never had a pool, and I could barely afford a tarp that year.

† It took me forever to get my pages like I like them. I hope it helped someone out there.

1000s that hold down the pool tarp, but I do recommend setting the backlight to "always on," which creates a nice ambiance in the evenings.

Q Did you always plan to win your first true pro race [the Tour de San Luís] to help with the sale of your new book, so you wouldn't have to live on $10 a day anymore?

Yes. I started this Bond-villain-style scheme in 2008 when I graduated from the University of Florida, where I studied English and journalism. That's when I set the goal of writing a book, signing to Garmin-Sharp, and winning my first professional race, to achieve the highest ratio of difficulty and physical discomfort to financial reward, greater meaning, and benefit to society. I've been in a tight race with rodeo clowns and ice sculptors, but I'm hoping that the book will put me over the edge and my daily allowance will improve.

Q What's the most flat tires you've ever gotten on a ride?

When it comes to flats, the limiting factor isn't how many flats one could possibly have, as much as it is about how many spare tubes one brings. I carry two tubes most days, three for rides if I expect lots of miles, dirt roads, and bad cell reception.

Once I get the second flat, I'm calling a friend to come pick me up, because let's face it, the ride is ruined. If I keep going, I'll probably get hit by a car. Does anyone keep riding after a second flat if they don't have to? If you have, what went through your mind? Did you really think it was going to turn into a pleasant spin from there? Was it a productive training day? Maybe you continued out of a sense of guilt, like you'd feel "soft" if you didn't complete the workout? I'd say you're tempting fate.

The line between perseverance and banging your head against a wall is a fine one. Wait. No, it's not. The line is two flats. Same thing when it comes to road rash. If you crash in a race, sure, keep going. But if you crash on a training ride, accept your fate and take the shortest route home. Don't go do intervals with your shorts all ripped up.*

And while we're at it, here's another good rule: If you start the day with a full charge on your iPhone and it runs out of juice, don't go looking for a charge. Leave it off. You're done.†

---

* I once crashed on a training ride, went home to change my shorts and clean my wounds, and then went back out to finish my intervals.

† I had to set this limit for myself on travel days. When I'm writing, my goal is to use up a full charge on my MacBook every day.

Q How much does your weight fluctuate throughout the year? When do you lose weight, and when do you just try to maintain? How do you choose your ideal race weight?

Most guys put on 5 to 10 pounds in the off-season, but I don't think anyone fluctuates more than that. The race season is spread out so much, you can never afford to be unfit. I don't go more than 5, because I would dread the effort required to lose it.

I only try to cut calories when I'm training. You set a weight target for an event, and whether you get there or not, once you're a couple days from the start, it's a lot more important to be fueled and ready to race than it is to be super skinny. I've heard of some guys using a stage race to lose weight, but I think most of us are too scared to bonk. If I cut calories at a race dinner, I'm sure I'd accidentally make the early break the next day and regret it.

To choose your ideal weight, a lot of riders just think, "If that was my best result, imagine how well I could have done if I was two pounds less!" I've had good results at 146 pounds, but great results at 152. The best method is to keep a training log and look back over all of your competitions to see what you weighed for your best ride. That should be your ideal weight. Pass the celery, please.

Q Have you ever had random cyclists race you on training rides?

Unfortunately, all pros have run-ins like that. Part of it is just the basic human urge to compete, so I understand when a kid on a BMX bike races me to the next block, but it's sad when adults can't restrain themselves. I once had a 40-year-old man drop his wife and kids to attack me for an hour on a bike path, on Christmas. I was training,* so I kept my heart rate to a strict coach-prescribed 140 beats per minute, while he shot past me on every hill and came back on the flats.

---

* I'm Jewish, so don't judge me for training on Christmas. On Christian holidays, the roads are mine.

I can only imagine the conversation when he got home: "I know we were just out for a nice ride together, and then I was late for Christmas dinner, but don't you understand that this was my big chance?"

Q Are there groupies in pro cycling?

Of course! I just got this new one from Shimano that's electric. You push a button, and it shifts gears! Wait, you said group-ies! My mistake.

My experience has been the opposite—cycling seems to be a turnoff to most women, based on this conversation, which I've had, or witnessed, about a million times:

Woman: "What do you do?"

Pro cyclist: "I race bikes."

Woman: "Oh, cool! Like motorcycles?"

Pro cyclist: "No, no. Bicycles. The ones you have to pedal."

Woman: "Oh, so you're doing tricks or flying through the woods?"

Pro cyclist: "No, I race road bikes, like in the Tour de France. I can almost do a wheelie."

Woman: "Why do you have to wear those tights?"

I haven't come across any cycling group-ies. If they did exist, they'd have a hard time getting through the crowd of middle-aged men drooling over my Cervélo with the electronic group-o.

Q I'm just getting into cycling. What would you recommend for a newbie?

That's great to hear! I remember how confusing it was when I started out, so I think I can help you avoid some of the pitfalls that I fell into. First, have a talk with your wife or girlfriend, and let her know you that you won't be seeing much of each other for a few years. If you have kids, take a picture of yourself so they don't forget what you look like, and upgrade your phone plan so you can call them between intervals. Next, if your place has white carpet, go ahead and paint black streaks on it. It's going to look like that from grease stains in a few months, so you might as well get it over with. Stock your bathroom with razors, gauze pads, and Tegaderm.

Finally, you'll need to rent a moving truck. Back it up to the loading dock at your nearest bike shop, and just tell the guy you want one of everything. You'll need it eventually, and this will save some time. Get more than one tube, though. Get a thousand tubes.

Q I'm 17 and a Cat. II racer. Should I go to college or quit school to race my bike full-time?

Well, that depends. How nice is your parents' basement? I actually get this question a lot.* It's like there are two routes to the WorldTour. Here's the traditional one: You start racing at 15, you go to a USA Cycling talent ID camp, then you're on the national team as a junior, on a pro development team like BISSELL as a U23, and when you get through that they toss you a two-year contract on a WorldTour team. It's easy, except you have to train your ass off, and most guys crack by 21.

The less-traditional route in this era was blazed by Ted King, followed by guys like me, Kiel Reijnen, and Chad Haga.

---

* After *Pro Cycling on $10 a Day* came out, I got a ton of e-mails from people who read a book filled with advice and then wanted personalized advice from me on top of it, instead of just getting to work. One said, "I did what you said in the books and dropped out of school to race bikes," which is certainly not what I said. I think he read it through a kaleidoscope.

We went to school full-time, had to convince our professors that they should let us miss class next week for something called "Redlands," and did as much racing as we could between semesters, joining domestic pro teams after we graduated. If we won enough in the U.S., made a good showing when we got a shot at a race such as the Tour of California, it made for a tough few years, but WorldTour teams eventually noticed.

Then there are guys who hedged their bets, like Ben King and Andrew Talansky. They both went to college and left early when they knew they could make it and school was costing them valuable watts. I tell kids that it's not all or nothing. If you missed out on making the national team, suck it up and go to school or get a part-time job. Don't act like doing 30 race days as an amateur is a full-time gig. You probably won't win the Tour de France like that, but you wouldn't anyway, and for every Tejay van Garderen or Talansky who's on that track—who made the right career call not to waste four years in college—there are 100 you haven't heard of who went and raced full-time before they had to and probably regret it now. Unless their parents have a nice basement.

Q When you're in a breakaway all day, do riders form a future friendship?

A breakaway can make a friend or an enemy, but rarely anything in between. I've always said that a long break is one of the best ways to get to know a person. Certain riders need to be in control, and they'll bark at you to slow down or speed up. Others will take their pulls and mind their own business. I've learned that the guy who gives you a sip of water will also hold the elevator door open when he sees you running down the hallway, and he'll give you the shirt off his back (not that you'd ever want his sweaty shirt). The one who's looking for excuses to skip his pulls, on the other hand, is most likely to crash you in the last turn, won't chip in for gas on the drive home, and should not be left alone with your girlfriend.

Q I get excited when I race, and it's difficult to unwind when it's over. Do you ever find it hard to sleep after a race?

Normally, a race tires me out enough that falling asleep isn't a problem. Or, the race is boring, and I never get excited to begin with. The only exception is when a race ends late in the day. I've experienced a few criterium series where I get home and calculate that if I was hit with a tranquilizer dart the minute I pulled into my driveway, I'd get four hours of sleep before I'd have to get up for the next race. That's probably why crit riders end up at bars after the finish.

Q How do you know when it's time to change a tire?

Tires are a funny thing—either they're perfectly fine or they're threadbare and in desperate need of replacement.

Of course, you want to maximize the miles you get from every tire, but if you try to stretch it too far, your punishment is an upper-body workout with your minipump, or fiddling with CO_2 cartridges until you screw them all up and then get an upper-body workout with a minipump that you borrow from one of your friends while they wait impatiently and roll their eyes at your tube-changing ineptitude. If you feel a flat spot on the rubber or you see a bunch of little rocks or bits of glass stuck in the cracks, get rid of the tire before a punctured tube forces that decision upon you.*

Whatever you do, when the tire is worn out, throw it away. Don't be the guy who has a box in his garage full of "almost dead" tires. Also, don't be a pain about matching

---

* Pro tip that never made it into a column: If you have a little cut but the tire is good otherwise, put a drop of Super Glue in there. Good to go!

the front and back ones. Sure, it doesn't look "pro" to have mismatched tires, but you don't look pro anyway, so you might as well save the money.

Q I've been training with power, trying to reach the numbers that pros do, but I seem to be a pure sprinter. Does a pro have "pro numbers" in threshold, sprints, and everything else, or are some guys only good at certain intensities?

You and I have the opposite problem, as I'm somewhat of a pure climber. The good news is that you don't need to have a huge threshold power if you're fast enough in the sprint. The bad news is that a sprinter does need enough endurance to make it to the end of the race, and then those last few minutes of fighting for position. And then you sprint. Or so I'm told.

I'm sure there are some pros with good numbers across the board, but the best sprinters can't climb anywhere near the best climbers, and if you put me in a velodrome with one of those big track dudes, I can go up the banking against anyone, but that's about it. You don't want to be incredibly weak in any part of your power numbers, so train your weaknesses, but you only need to be great at one thing to win races.

Q I'm an amateur racer, so I travel most weekends to small races and I don't make much in prize money. I try to stay with friends or host housing to keep it cheap, but I end up at a lot of motels. How do you choose the ideal hotel or motel for a bike racer on the cheap? How do you eat healthy in these situations?

Even when you make it as a pro (and I know you will, because you're asking the right questions), hotels are hit-or-miss. Every time I enter the room for the first time, I like to pretend my agent called ahead to meet my strict requirements, so I

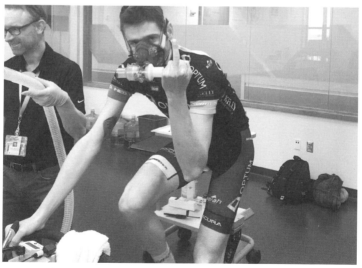
Lactate threshold testing.

tick off an imaginary checklist: "Yep, the towels are folded. Mmm-hmm, the pillows are on the bed, just like I said." It starts things off on the right foot, because like it or not, that's where you're sleeping.

I've noticed that hotels are an economic anomaly: The more you pay, the less you get. For example, if you get a room at the Hyatt for $400 a night, you pretty much have the same bed, desk, and bathroom, but the Wi-Fi will probably cost you an extra $15, the buffet breakfast could run another $20, and there's no minifridge.

On the other end of the spectrum, a room for $50 a night is tempting, but they have their downsides, like drunk people being rowdy in the hallway at 2 a.m., or a drug deal gone wrong in the next room, and now you're going to the emergency room with wounds from a stray bullet (those walls are paper-thin), which is less-than-ideal race prep. Also, beware the "free breakfast" in these cases, which is probably warm coffee out of Styrofoam cups, non-dairy creamer, and donuts salvaged from a Dumpster.

The sweet spot hotel for an up-and-coming bike racer is in the $65- to $90-per-night range. This is your Holiday Inn Express, your Red Roof Inn, Motel 6 (stay away from the Motel 5.8), and Travelodge. With the big chain hotels, you get a certain level of cleanliness and decency, because they can't afford a lawsuit. You can always count on free Wi-Fi, a mini-fridge, and a microwave. Sometimes, breakfast at these places is acceptable, but I always like to pack what I call a "homeless kitchen." This is a cooler with a container of cooked rice, some fruits and veggies, and eggs, along with a few packets of oatmeal, an electric burner, a blender for post-race recovery shakes, a small pot, a skillet, dishes and silverware, a sponge, and a small bottle of olive oil. It's only a little depressing, and it'll get you through the weekend cheap.

If you're too lazy for a homeless kitchen, I've had some of my best races on a Waffle House breakfast, and here's a pro tip: Almost every town has a Thai restaurant, where you can get a cheap, high-carb, nutritious meal, which beats room service at the Hyatt every time.

Q Do cyclists abstain from sex before events? I've heard that sex affects testosterone levels and can hurt performance.

Yes, but only if "abstain" means "we don't have sex because no one wants to date a dude with shaved legs who mostly lives in a bus and marginal hotels."*

---

* Original answer that was too distasteful for print: "Sure we do! I abstained the sheets just last night."

Q Pro cyclists are in different countries almost every week. What do you do for a phone plan? Do teams provide cell phones?

I hear that Sky riders get cell phones and laptops, but I think they're the only ones.* The rest of us have to handle our own, and some do it better than others. I won't tell you who,† but one friend claims to have paid over 100,000 euros in fees to Vodafone over the last few years. Others carry multiple phones, or an envelope full of SIM cards, like skinny spies with shaved legs and bad tans. I opted for one phone with unlimited international data and texting,‡ so it's great as long as you don't want to actually call anyone, and who calls anyone these days? Sky riders, I suppose.

Q Should ex-dopers be allowed to attend charity rides and gran fondos?

If a guy is banned or suspended, of course he shouldn't race, but as Moses chiseled into the Bill of Rights, "Thou

---

* And I think it's because their team is spying on them.

† Thomas Dekker.

‡ From a guy who normally hates everything: T-Mobile International is actually a good deal.

shalt not disallow any man from riding his bike with friends."

The problem is that any time you get a pack of cyclists together for a ride, someone makes it a "race." I read a few angry Internet posts about Levi Leipheimer winning an event called "Crusher in the Tushar" over the summer, how he was taking prize money and opportunities away from clean riders. It's always frustrating to lose, but I'm pretty sure that whatever prize money Levi won wouldn't buy him a bottle of scalp aftershave, and no one's getting contracts from winning unsanctioned dirt road races, even if they do have catchy, rhyming names. If anything, Levi's attendance might help an aspiring pro, because no matter how hard the event is, beating a pack of weekend warriors doesn't impress anybody. But if you can beat Levi, sponsors might notice.

I do wonder why events invite those guys. They might bring media attention, but having Lance show up to your benefit ride would be like inviting a serial killer to an NRA event. Sure, he's a good shot and he's famous, but that's probably not the image you want. On the other hand, if Lance invites himself to your ride, well, now it depends on your interpretation of Moses. And try to have a catchy, rhyming name.

Q I keep seeing riders complain about having to race in bad weather, wanting stages to be shortened or cancelled because of cold, heat, or rain. When did pro cyclists turn into such wussies, and what can we do about it? Fans love the drama and crashes.

Indeed, the wussification of pro cyclists is a growing concern. These cowards seem to think that doing six-hour training rides, spending months away from home, and choking down overcooked pasta at hotel buffets is enough to earn them their exorbitant paychecks. And now they don't want to race in conditions that would harm their long-term health? The nerve!

You've pointed out riding conditions, but I've seen other examples of wussiness lately, which I think we also need to address:

- Riders who wear helmets.

- Riders who need saddles, because the seatpost isn't soft enough.

- Riders who don't drill the cleat directly into their foot, opting instead to use a cowardly "shoe" device.

- Riders who use mitts when removing a soufflé from the oven.

On second thought, maybe pro cyclists have been through enough. Now that they're not all on EPO, the race organizers could shorten a stage here or there, rather than trying to out-epic each other, and fans that want to see more blood can go watch a rodeo or UFC.

Q **If you could give one piece of advice to a young cyclist who aspires to go pro, what would it be?**

You should probably ask for more than one piece of advice. If you need it all summarized in one bullet point, it's not going to happen for you. If I had to pick one: Make sure you're getting the right advice. I've met a lot of coaches, bike fitters, and team managers who don't know what the hell they're talking about.* Find someone who's achieved a level that you want to reach, harass them with questions, and when you're as good as they are, find someone better to harass. I'd say you can ask me here, but if you ask one question a month, you won't have enough answers until you're racing the masters 50+ category.

---

* I still have PTSD from watching an ex-girlfriend get a bike fit once.

Q Is it difficult to adjust to riding different bikes when you change teams or sponsors?

It's always a little confusing when you drive someone else's car, right? You know how to drive, so you can get around, but you keep turning on the windshield wipers when you're looking for the headlights, and you might pull up to the wrong side of the pump at the gas station. Riding a new bike is basically the same thing, so any time a pro changes teams, there's adjustment to be made.

First, you have to deal with the fit. Your old bike had a 56-cm top tube with a 100-mm stem, but your new bike's top tube is 55.4 cm. You can either swing by the bike shop and demand a 106-mm stem to make up the difference, or fudge your shifters around and get used to it.

Next, when you switch saddles, it's not hard to get the height and fore/aft positions where you want them, but then you sit on each saddle a little differently, you think about it too much, and suddenly you're stopping at every light and busting out the multitool.

It took me a long time, but a million bike fits and trial and error got me to a position that I like, and now when I get a new bike, I take it to a bike fitter. I don't ask for a fit, but they help me match my angles and position to what they measured on my old bike. Then, I get a massage a couple days after I change something (even just installing new cleats), and that goes a long way toward working out the kinks.

Most importantly, don't be a damn princess (or wussy) who needs everything within 0.5 nanometers. I've seen pros mark their seatpost where they want it, and then purposely move it up and down every few rides so it's a bit off. It's impossible to get exact matches on your training bike, your race bike, your spare bike, and the bike that you take from your domestique when the shit hits the fan (or the ass hits the cobbles), and you'll need to be able to win on all of them. So, there's your answer. But I still can't find the turn signal on my new Diamondback.

Q How do you stay motivated through long miles, hard workouts, or bad weather?

If you're a cyclist, but you suddenly find that riding is a chore, you probably need a break. I can't remember the last time I looked at my bike and didn't want to go pedal around on it. Of course, I'm a bike racer, and I also can't remember what month it is. In fact, where am I?

I can sympathize about bad weather, though. It's tough to look out the window at snow or rain and know you have to fight through it, but mostly, it's about clothing and gear. If you have enough gloves, shoe covers, and fenders, you can stay comfortable in just about any conditions, but my solution to bad weather is simpler: I move. One winter, I survived a couple of months in Baltimore and then finally drove down to Florida instead of fighting through an upcoming blizzard. Call me soft, but if you've been a bike racer as long as I have, the last thing you need is to harden up.

Nowadays, I live in Los Angeles, which is experiencing a severe drought. It bodes horribly for the environment and future generations, but it's great if you like riding in just a jersey and shorts.* The best part? When the weather is warm year-round, you don't even need to know what month it is.

Q What's the weirdest thing about pro cycling?

The whole concept of pro cycling is crazy when you think about it: I'm better at riding a bike than 99.9 percent of the

---

* Also: great restaurants.

people in my neighborhood,* so I jump on a plane to meet up with a bunch of guys in the top 0.01 percent in their neighborhoods so we can see who's the very fastest.

It's best not to think about the big picture, though, so I focus on bodily functions. The weirdest thing about my job is the amount of public urination that is required. We try to be discreet, but there just aren't enough restrooms out there. I'm sure thousands of cars have passed me taking a nature break on training rides, with my back to the road. I'm always afraid that I'll get caught, and I can only hope that the police officer also has a bladder and sympathizes with my plight.[†]

Q I see a lot of racers crowd-funding specific races or trips. Why should I pay for some kid to go race in Belgium?

When I was a kid, my mom and dad would buy me a cookie at the mall food court. I'm sure I appreciated their generosity, but when I was old enough, they gave me $3 a week to

---

* 99.9! I'm so hard on myself! I think it's safe to say that I'm the best bike racer in Toluca Lake, California.

† I pee in public twice a day on average, which is a crime. There's the urban legend of someone who knows a guy who knows a guy who had to register as a sex offender for it, which would have to mean there's at least one cop and one judge with no bladder, in a town with no real crime. Or he was peeing on a school or something.

do chores around the house. I should have called child protective services and reported them for labor law violations, but instead, I bought a cookie with my own money that I'd worked and sweated for. I'll never forget how that cookie looked, felt, and tasted when I had earned it.

When I was coming up in cycling, teammates and I worked side jobs, from coaching to bartending—even writing silly books and magazine articles. And when we were struggling in a race, we dug deeper because of what it took just to get there. I think there's something to be said for earning your way and paying for your own cookie, rather than having it given to you. Or maybe we wouldn't have been struggling if someone gave us money and we could put our feet up instead of working.*

In the grand scheme of things, you'd be doing more good if you fund a campaign to bring water to a village in Africa,† but if a stranger on the Internet will get a vicarious thrill out of watching these riders try not to crash in Belgium,

---

* I'm editing this in an election year, so this rant sounds almost political. I do wonder if I would have started a crowd-fund if that existed during Part 1 of this book. Pride is a luxury, and I was desperate to be a bike racer. I stayed at a lot of people's houses for free, but I never took cash.

† Or to my thirsty village of Los Angeles, California.

and that's the way people want to spend their money, more power to them—and more Belgian chocolate and waffles (hopefully they're not buying beers)* to the beneficiaries.

Anyway, my paycheck just showed up. If anyone needs me, I'll be eating cookies at the mall.

Q **I know it's good to get a massage after a hard workout, but everywhere I go it's candles and classical music, and they hardly touch my legs. Do you get massages when you're not with your team? How do I find a good masseuse?**

Most pros try to get a massage at least once a week when they're training, but it is hard to find the right person, and it's quite a risk to pay $75 or more for what might be a bad massage. I've had folks do nothing but squeeze my shoulders for an hour, despite repeated reminders that "I really don't use any muscles above the waist."

Sometimes they get to the legs, but they're so weak that you barely feel it. Or worse: They go too hard, like they're trying to kill you through your hamstrings, and you feel like

---

* One of the American amateurs who does an annual "Follow my dreams" crowd-fund posts a lot of pictures from after-parties and I want to kill him for it.

you were just tackled by the police after a long pursuit, and they're pinning you down while they wait for backup.

In most cycling-friendly areas, you can find someone who's worked for a team on a part-time basis and sees clients when they're home; or there might be one sports massage specialist who works with all the cyclists in the area. Find the fastest racer in your neighborhood and ask for a recommendation. If that doesn't work out, rob a liquor store and let the cops pin you down. It might be a rough massage, but the price is right.

Q Disc brakes: yea or nay?

I say nay to disc brakes, not because I'm afraid of hot, spinning meat-slicers cutting open my spleen in a crash or because I'm afraid that I'll slam on my disc brakes and everyone with caliper brakes will uncontrollably slam into my back. I say nay because I hate technology, progress, and change.*

Speaking of "nay," I have to go hook up my horse and buggy. We're headed to Circuit City to find a new cassette player, and then I need to fix my typewriter.

---

* This was the big debate in spring 2015. Everyone was asking, but I had to dodge the question because I was scared of sponsors getting mad at me. I give an honest answer later.

Q **I recently crashed after swerving to avoid a stray dog. What is the largest animal that you have seen someone run over and still manage to stay upright? Was the animal harmed?**

I once bunny-hopped a dead armadillo. I did him no harm. Midrace, I've run over arms, legs, and one neck of many humans, in panicked efforts to stay upright. They were harmed, but not so much by me, and it wasn't on purpose.

The most harm I've seen is done to riders' sunglasses after a crash. Sunglasses are always thrown clear in a crash, and it's sort of a game to dodge the body and crush the glasses. Rude, I know, but the folks I race with get their glasses for free.

Q **Is there a race on the calendar where all the competitors agree to race completely drunk? That would be awesome.**

This is a stupid question, so what does it say about me that I have an answer? At collegiate mountain bike nationals, there used to be an unsanctioned "naked crit." That's probably the closest you'll come to a drunk race, but as I understand it, Tramadol isn't far off, and some teams still use that in races. A few months ago, my 84-year-old grandmother started taking Tramadol for pain. We had a fight about it and she was kicked out of the Movement for Credible Cycling, which doesn't allow Tramadol, among other things. Then she stopped because it made her too loopy, and Grandma couldn't concentrate on her puzzles. Something tells me that if Tramadol made it hard for Granny to pick out the corner pieces, riders might be impaired ripping through corners on wet cobblestones. Awesome, right?

Q Do you work on your own bikes?

At races, the team mechanics handle that for us, but at home, I like to know how to work on my own bike, because a professional should understand his equipment. I think I do a decent job of it, but if you said that to anyone who works at the bike shops I frequent in my neighborhood, they'd never stop laughing. They might also share a story about when I showed up with my rear wheel jammed into the front fork, or a derailleur screwed into my thumb.*

Q How does your girlfriend deal with you being gone for long training camps and stage races?

---

* Shout-out to Troy, Steve, and Rob at H&S Bikes, Jared at Velo Studio, and so many others over the years.

When I leave home, she climbs into a cryogenic freezer, preserved until my return. Okay, that's not true, but it would be cool if I could afford it. We just have a regular freezer, which wouldn't be comfortable. She goes about her business, we talk on the phone, and I'm sure there's plenty of upside to having me out of the house, such as peace and quiet, fewer grease stains on the sofa, and, of course, the leftovers don't disappear out of the (non-cryogenic) freezer so fast.*

Q Do riders always obey their team directors? Have you ever gone rogue and hatched your own plan? What's the punishment if a rider goes against the team?

Back in the old days of race radios, there were a couple times when I pulled out the earpiece and claimed that it wasn't working, but I don't think I ever blatantly disobeyed my team. Like any job, if you have a specific task, and you decide to do something else, you're fired pretty quick. Unless you go rogue and you win, in which case the director will applaud your effort and act like whatever you did was his idea.

---

* This one didn't work out.

If you screw up really bad, here's your plan C: I've noticed that you can get dropped and finish minutes behind, but if you wheelie across the finish line, all is forgiven.*

Q What do you think about riders having RVs at races instead of staying at hotels?[†]

I see why teams might see potential for marginal gains with an RV. It's not as if riders are carrying their own bags up and down stairs, but removing the step of packing or digging for your toothbrush is appealing, as is having the space to bring everything you want, rather than just what you can fit in a suitcase.

What they might be forgetting is that riders aren't robots, and one of the best things about racing is hanging out with your teammates in a hotel room, watching "The Simpsons" in whatever language, or sitting on the soigneur's bed gobbling cereal, making fun of whoever's getting a massage.

A little extra rest sounds great, but at least for me, it wouldn't be worth the trade-off. I remember how stressful it was to be in the leader's yellow jersey at the Tour de San

---

* I never learned how to wheelie.

† This was a big debate when Richie Porte brought an RV to the Giro.

Luis; having Tyler Farrar to joke around with in my hotel room made it much easier. If I had my own room, I'd be constantly texting friends to come hang out, and that was just a little race. I can't imagine the pressure and stress that would come along with trying to win a Grand Tour. Maybe that's why I've never won a Grand Tour. Well, I can think of at least two other reasons (power and weight).

I'm not surprised that the UCI would rule against it—not that they don't have better things to address, but if this caught on, it'd be a slippery slope finding parking for an extra 200 RVs.

Q What interview question are you most tired of?

Fans and media love asking some form of "How hard is that climb?" They want you to say that the climb in their race or neighborhood is the hardest, steepest, and longest you've ever done, but I have news for you: Plenty of climbs are hard, and the big ones are all about the same.* Sure, they might each have their own personality, but even the worst

---

* The narrative of races all claiming that they're the "toughest" is just bad marketing.

city planners try not to pave roads that are over 15 percent. So start there, add in a few steeper pitches, bad pavement, maybe some weather, and that's as tough as it gets. "Hardest climb in the world" is a 500-way tie.

What makes a climb hard in a race isn't the climb—it's who you're racing against and what the race situation is. Alpe d'Huez is impossible if you're the guy trying to hang with Contador, but it's cake in the grupetto.

Q For lowly U.S. amateurs, it's pretty much all about criterium racing. What are Phil's criterium racing secrets to success?

Scrub your road rash with a bristly brush to get the dirt and debris out, and use antibiotic ointment to prevent infection. The only bandage that works is 3M's Tegaderm. If you can't afford that, just tape Saran Wrap around the affected area. Clean and change the dressing every day.* Always travel with a spare derailleur hanger and helmet.

Q What's a product that pros might buy on their own, regardless of sponsorship?

---

* If the U.S. Criterium series ended, stock in 3M would plummet.

I've been training in SoCal heat lately, so the first thing that comes to mind is oversized water bottles. Teams usually provide the standard 20-ouncer, but you can find bigger ones, which means less stopping and fewer dollars wasted at gas stations.*

While I try to save you money, a better pro might recommend a sports car and a condominium in Monaco.

Q A masters racer in my area was suspended for using EPO a few years ago. Now he's back in the races. Should I be okay with that?

Doping is wrong whether you're a pro or an amateur, but I think dopers in the professional ranks and dopers in the masters categories are grapefruits and oranges. (Not apples and oranges. They're close enough to both be in the citrus family.)

Pros will probably return to whatever pays the bills after they're suspended. They'll know that they'll have to deal with hate from fans and riders, but you can't exactly blame them as long as the rules allow them to race again. A masters racer (or

---

* CamelBak makes one that's insulated, 36 oz. You can go all day on two of those bad boys.

even an amateur) returning after a suspension is confusing, because I'm sure it's no fun to sit in a pack of dudes who don't want you there, and he's not in it for the money. Why not use the two-year "vacation" to get into ultramarathons instead, or maybe something dangerous, like BASE jumping? Or perhaps this racer is approaching an age where Scrabble would be more appropriate.

Basically, welcome to cycling. You get to judge and decide who you want to be friends with, and then be judged for that. The best part: There's no right answer! Before you complain, understand that my answer here is going to result in hate mail that says, "You're too easy on the dopers" and hate mail that says, "You're too hard on the dopers." (Also, try racing in Europe with a tattoo that says "CLEAN.")

Q What's the best cycling-related purchase you've ever made?

I had eyeglasses since first grade. My eyes got irritated when I wore contacts, so for my first couple years as a racer, I had to deal with prescription sunglasses, sorting out new lenses with a team's sunglasses sponsor, which could change from year to year. One off-season, I finally spent $3,000 on Lasik surgery.

As far as investments go, carbon wheels and power meters are great, but they're much better if you can see them. The second-best purchase was custom insoles. I have two pairs that have lasted since 2008. I don't let them out of my laser-enhanced sight, and I think I'll have to retire when they wear out.

Q I've been having knee problems, but every bike fitter I see gives me different advice. I thought this was a science. Who's right?

Ah, bike fitters. I've had many bad experiences but also a couple good ones. The guy at your local bike shop might not know what he's doing, but he always tells you he's the best. You should start with someone who's had some sort of certification or training, and has the equipment to do it right.

Watch out if:

- *They try to sell you something.* Maybe you would be better off with a longer stem, but it's also a conflict of interest if they're profiting from selling it to you.

- *They offer weird solutions.* Be wary if they say you need all sorts of wedges or spacers, or one pedal longer than the other. There are people with weird physiologies who do need that stuff, but most of the time, I think they're getting fancy to impress you.

- *They try to fix what ain't broke.* Have you ever hired a contractor to fix your toilet, and on the way through your kitchen he asks what idiot installed your cabinets? They all do that, and a lot of bike fitters have the same attitude. If you feel good and go fast, but they tell you to change everything, they're probably steering you in the wrong direction.

- *They always know more than you do.* You should have input in your bike fit. Sure, they're the experts, but you know your body. I've seen fitters who refuse to fit a certain brand of saddle, for example. You should be working with the fitter, not getting bossed around.

Once you find a fitter you trust, remember that it's a process. If something is wrong, go back and work on it before you try another fitter and start from scratch. Also, see my previous answer about insoles. Custom insoles can prevent a lot of problems.

Q Do you litter bottles and wrappers during a race?

I try my best to wait until I'm in the feed zone or near a spectator to toss a bottle, and I usually cram wrappers into a pocket. Sometimes, when a race is on, you have to react and don't have time to stuff your pockets, or you simply drop what you're holding. As much as I'd love to see my director's face if I turned around to retrieve an errant Clif gel, I'll admit that I have littered in my time, but I follow simple advice that Jeremy Powers gave me, and I encourage you to join us: For every item you have to litter, pick up two later. As long as you don't forget, you're trash-negative.

I also encourage clubs and teams to sign up for local Adopt-a-Highway programs, as the University of Florida team did when I went to school there. If you bring a good crew, it's almost fun to pick up trash for a day. It's also a great learning experience, because you see all the liquor bottles in the grass, which gives you a better understanding of just how many folks are driving drunk on your favorite roads—good to remember on days that you don't feel like wearing a helmet.

Q **I have a giant patch of road rash, and it's taking forever to heal. How does a pro handle an injury like this?**

I wish I weren't such an expert in this department, but through a combination of personal experience and watching television, I'm sure I know enough to help.

First, when you're lying there on the pavement, look around and figure out who's responsible. Who crashed with you? Can you blame them? Who was driving the motorcycle? Who put a dangerous corner in the race? Who caused it to rain? Who dug that pothole? A flat tire can be a great scapegoat. Maybe it tore when you slid for 30 feet and rammed into a wall, but if there's nothing else, you can always claim that you suddenly flatted in the middle of a corner. Nothing you can do about that, right? Just remember that a true pro never takes responsibility for a crash.

After you get up and dust yourself off, wait for the cameras to crowd around, pretend you're calm and collected, and then hurl your bike into the woods! Your sponsors deserve this disrespect for making a product that's subject to harmful forces like gravity, friction, and momentum. Don't forget your helmet and glasses. Spike those in the end zone.

Get back on the spare bike and hold onto the medical car as long as you need to while the race doctor cleans

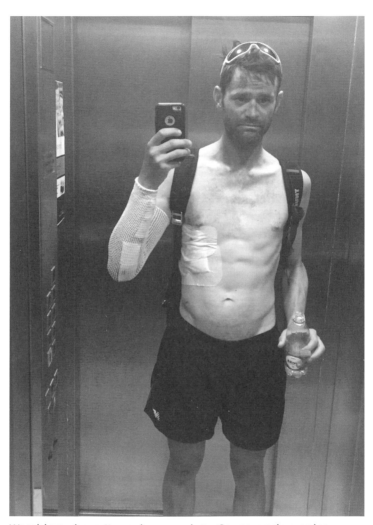

Watching where I'm going: 0 points. Gauze work: 1 point.

you up. You'll return to the pack completely cleaned and bandaged half an hour later, with one arm several inches longer than the other.

I estimate that up to 25 percent of cyclists don't have a doctor in a follow car on training rides. When that's the case, I've been very successful at entering the shower—still wearing my torn and bloody kit—and scrubbing the hell out of my wounds with tons of soap and water, using the torn chamois I'm about to throw away.

To kill the germs, liberally pour various chemicals into the wound. (If it's not stinging, it's not working.)

If you're not crying yet, throw some of the chemicals into your eyes.

While you're still in the shower, make sure you scream and groan in pain for anyone within earshot. That way it's clear that you held it back for all those hours, and listeners will admire your strength and pain threshold while feeling sorry for you.

Cover the wound with Tegaderm. It's expensive, but nothing else works on a large area. Everyone buys five different products for $2 each, throws them out, and then spends $6 on the good stuff. You should skip the first part.

Now that you've had time to think about it, log in to your Twitter account and start publicly blaming the guilty parties.

Inspect your helmet. If there's a crack in it, you need a new one. It's oddly satisfying to jump up and down on it, or run over it with a rental car. Have fun with it. Don't let that concussion sap your creativity!

If you're at a hotel, ruin as many towels and sheets as you can and move on. If you're at home, keep a set of maroon linens in the closet for just these occasions.

Q **I find myself going through play-by-play breakdowns of group rides with my friends. As a pro, do you ever overhear conversations like this? How dumb do we sound?**

Imagine how a NASA engineer might feel if you told him a long story about the balsa wood model airplane you've been working on.

Q **I'm amazed at how many pros drop out of races when they're out of contention. I understand the rationale for this (40th and 40 minutes down on the winner isn't much different from a DNF, and dropping out would help recovery), but do pros ever get annoyed at quitting**

a one-day race or the last day of a stage race, even if they're no longer a factor? You guys are presumably super-competitive, and I imagine not finishing is frustrating.

Pros are very competitive, but about winning, not finishing. If you've just started racing, or you're using a smaller race to train for a more important one, finishing matters, but once you know you're capable of making it to the end, you don't really need to prove it. If you were told to do a job other than win—as 80 percent of pros are—and that job is done, sure, it's best to cruise in slow to the finish, but sometimes getting off the bike early and being first to shower and put your feet up is a victory in itself.

One of my first European races was a three-stage race, and the final stage ended with short laps around a city. I was a few minutes down and wanted to finish, but then I passed the bus with a lap to go and noticed the mechanics packing bikes and loading a trailer, which reminded me that we had an early flight and that it was going to be a rush to make it to the airport. I dropped out, because the best thing I could have done for my team was not to finish 80th but to make sure we were on time to the airport.*

---

* We missed the flight anyway. If I was really last, they would have all blamed me.

Pro cycling is a competition, but it's also a job. If you install car doors at a factory all day, when you've finished your last one, do you follow the car down the line until it's finished, or would your employers rather you clock out and go home to rest so you can do it again tomorrow?

Q You live in a city. Isn't it harder to train there? How do you deal with motorists?

I used to live in the South. Once, in Florida, a police car passed me and my friend on a ride, then pulled over and waited for us.

"You guys know it's against the law to ride side-by-side?" he asked. (If you read the news, it's no surprise that even the cops don't know the laws in Florida.)

"Actually, it's legal to ride side-by-side, as long as you're not impeding traffic," I replied.

"Well, y'all were impeding traffic."

"How'd you get past us, then?"

The cop let us keep riding, but how can you expect the average driver to know the laws if the police don't?

In rural areas, any attempt at standing up for yourself is a risk, because you don't want to lose a fight to a guy in a pickup truck, miles from anywhere.

So honestly, I feel safer riding in the city. I moved to Los Angeles two years ago, and I've never had a scary interaction here. Why the discrepancy? I don't think people in the city are any less ignorant, but they don't stop to argue, because there are more witnesses around and they actually have something to do. Maybe LA has more cars to honk at you, but then it's over. Also, on country roads, cars go fast. In the city, the speed is more reasonable.

Q I'm a junior. Do you have any advice that might help me? How do I stay skinny?

Well, Junior, I'm the wrong person to ask, because I didn't race until I was 19. If you follow my footsteps through the youth ranks, you'll compete in the state yo-yo champion-ships, play Counter-Strike on your computer for a few years, and get most of your calories from Coca-Cola. Then you'll look in the mirror when you're 18, quit all of that, and ride a bike to undo it.

Actually, that wouldn't be a bad route at all, except that you could probably do better than Counter-Strike these days. I assure you, though: Yo-yos will never go out of style. Friends might make fun of you at first, but then you show them a few tricks, and they're impressed.

I'd recommend you don't start racing until you're fully grown. I've been the same height since I started riding, and I still struggle to get my saddle height where I want it. And definitely don't worry about your weight as a junior. Don't get fat, but it's better to focus on improving your power than lowering your weight. When you get to an age when the power starts to creep down, that's when you count calories and work on the other side of the power-to-weight ratio.

From what I've seen, the guys who make it to the very top start young, win national championships at age 14, and they never stop. Look at results from the men's junior nationals from 5 to 10 years ago, and you'll see a lot of names like Tejay van Garderen, Lawson Craddock, Nate Brown, and Ian Boswell—all WorldTour riders today, but you'll also see a lot of dudes who quit by the age of 20 because they worked too hard and it wasn't fun anymore. Race a lot, enjoy yourself, and don't take it too seriously. Lawson, Nate, and Ian still don't. Tejay is serious sometimes, but we don't hold it against him.

Q **Pros are constantly changing bikes and equipment sponsors, or just getting new stuff after a crash, for**

example. How do you get all of your bikes to measure the same?

If you break a frame and replace it with the same one, you can take shortcuts,* like yanking your seatpost and bars from the old frame, instead of setting up a new bike from scratch.

When sponsors change, it's just about being thorough and doing the math before you pull on the bib shorts. If you go from a pedal with a 1-mm stack height to a pedal with 3 mm of stack, you raise the seatpost 2 mm. Then you chisel those measurements into three redundant stone tablets, give one to your team mechanic, carry one with you at all times (even to the bathroom), and put one in a vault, guarded by a dragon and at least two magic spells.

You have to be adaptable, because no one likes the guy who makes the group wait while he busts out the Allen wrench, moves his seat an imperceptible amount, and then announces it's "much better." I'll never be exactly right, so you should be able to be comfortable within a small range.†

---

* Bike racers knew more about shortcuts in the '90s, but we still have a few.

† If that's not a metaphor for life, I don't know what is.

Q I understand that, as a pro, you'll never clean or work on your own bike, but how do you deal with a squeaky chain?

I turn up the volume on my earphones.*

Q Is it cool or uncool to leave your old race numbers on for training?

When I started racing, I remember thinking girls in my dorm building might notice the race numbers. They'd think, "He's not just a guy that walks around in tights: he's serious. He might even be a winner." Then I realized that the folks I'd actually be training with were all at the same collegiate race I'd come from. They knew that I was not a winner—that I had gotten dropped from the break in the road race and finished fourth.†

The first time I used a frame number was similar. I left it on for one ride after the under-23 national championships that year (I DNFed) and was immediately called out by my friend David Guttenplan, who explained that having the number 37 electrical-taped to my seatpost was, in fact,

---

* I did a few weeks training alone with my headphones, and then I went out to ride with teammates (so no headphones) and noticed my training bike was making all sorts of noises.

† Georgia Tech road race, 2005: The day I learned about tactics.

not cool, even though it indicated that I'd competed at a big race. The lesson I learned then was that the truly cool don't have to advertise, and I followed that logic for eight years of racing.

But then something changed: I did bigger races, competed in more of them, and lived in Europe. When it came to cycling, I officially achieved "cool" status (or at least, "nothing to prove on the group ride" status). So I have no need to advertise, except that after a WorldTour race, the mechanic throws my bike in a bag with the frame number still on it. Removing it would require a screwdriver, 11 seconds, and "working on my bike," and since I'm a pro—as mentioned above—those are hurdles I can't get over. So until somebody does it for me, from now until I go back to the amateurs, the frame number stays.

The team also handles laundry when you're on the road, so it's pretty easy to grab your only clean jersey for a training ride and notice your number is still there from the last race. Most of the time, I'll take a minute and remove it, but maybe I'm tired, or maybe I'm only riding for an hour. By the end of August, you'll see numbers from the Vuelta at coffee shops all over Europe.

Is that cool? The only way to know is to ask the girls from my freshman dorm.

Q Everyone harasses me on the local group ride because I don't like to wear a helmet. But I raced many years back when nobody wore them. Shouldn't I be exempt from this rule?

That's like not wearing a seatbelt because your first car was a Model T, or refusing to wear a condom because you were having sex before the AIDS epidemic.

Every group ride has one annoying guy to gang up on, and he generally deserves it. Usually he blows through traffic lights or shows off on descents. On my group ride, there's a guy who wears his bright green argyle and rides a matching Cannondale. He goes hard on all the climbs and gets cussed out every week.

It sounds like you're "that guy" on your local ride. I'm not going to be much support when it comes to the helmet, because I think if you want to ride in a group, you should respect their standards. So buy a helmet, stop at the lights, and maybe even wear a condom.

Q How do you stay skinny? Do you have any diet hacks? Does Cannondale allow you to eat gluten?

When I was 17, a doctor told me I was obese, which meant I'd reached 25 percent body fat—and it also helped me understand why girls weren't talking to me. So I started riding my bike 9 miles each way to school. For breakfast, I'd have a chicken biscuit and a sweet tea from Chick-fil-A, and I'd try not to eat again for the rest of the day. I'm not suggesting you try that method, but after a few months, I lost 40 pounds and I had to spend all my allowance on new pants.

Now that I'm in the WorldTour, I do better than chicken biscuits. The team supplies me with all sorts of proteins and superfood powder to throw into my blender, and they have a nutrition consultant on staff. He chatted with my personal nutritionist in Los Angeles and approved the daily meal plan we'd been using: lots of veggies, good fats, different sources of animal protein, and then we add carbs based on how much I'm riding.

I'd post Dr. Goglia's meal plan here, but everybody's different, and then he wouldn't be able to sell it to Kanye West and the other celebrities he works with.* (It's known that Kanye reads *VeloNews*.)

I've found it easier to focus on what I have to eat, rather than what I can't. For example, I must drink three liters

---

* One of the many reasons I love Los Angeles is that I frequently see people I know on E!

of water every day (sparkling, because I'm a Euro-pro) and I must consume an entire bag of chopped kale or spinach. The greens go in my eggs with breakfast, in a shake after my ride, and in a salad at dinner. When you're full of leafy greens and water, you don't crave donuts so much (also, your bowel movements are like German trains—enormous and loud).

Here are some other tips that I've gathered from skinny teammates and friends in the WorldTour:

- If you're trying to lose weight, buy some small bowls and silverware. When the plate looks full, you feel full. At least, it works for us, because pro cyclists are great at fooling themselves. ("This race was bad, but I'll win the next one!")

- If you crave sugary cereal or junk food, you can always dilute it. For example, go with a 50-50 mixture of Corn Flakes and Frosted Flakes. It tastes the same. I have noticed that Cannondale no longer offers sugary cereals in the food room like it did in 2014, but if someone hands me a cookie (hint, hint), the team won't slap it out of my hand (there's a "cookie clause" in my contract).

When I raced in the U.S., I ran from gluten like it was Ebola, but then I found myself at a training camp in Mallorca, watching in horror as Dutch teammate Dylan van Baarle pounded a huge stack of white bread and butter at breakfast. We did some motor-pacing that day, and he attacked the car. I've since read studies saying that gluten is a factor for only a very limited number of athletes, but I didn't need research to know that. Dylan was enough.

I had to find the right resources and advice, and it took time to force myself into good habits, but now that I'm used to it, it's not a struggle to stay skinny like it was in high school. Girls still don't talk to me, though. Maybe I should take a shower.

Q What's a pro's biggest fear at a bike race? Are you afraid to crash? To lose?

Crashing sucks, but my biggest fear is forgetting my shoes. I've ridden Mavic shoes for years, I have custom insoles that I guard with my life, and the cleats are set up just like I like them. I can break my bike, or the airline could lose my clothing, and Vaughters will find more argyle for me. If a pro loses his shoes, though, it's over. You know how when you stand up, you check for your keys, wallet, and phone? Pro cyclists open our backpacks every few minutes to make sure the shoes are still there.*

Q What's the first thing you learned in a WorldTour race?

My WorldTour education actually began at sign-in, before my first race even started. On smaller teams, we'd head to sign-in whenever they were ready for us, but on Cannondale, we never go to sign-in alone, like women going to the restroom on a double date.

Q At races, do riders get their own hotel rooms? If you share, how do you decide who your roommate is?

Riders do share hotel rooms at races. The only exception is if you get sick. If you ever feel like getting your own room on a WorldTour team, just cough once in front of the team doctor. He'll go into full panic mode, and you'll be quarantined in no time.

I wouldn't be surprised if guys like Chris Froome have it in their contract to get a room to themselves, but most of us would end up in an insane asylum if we didn't have someone to speak with (for me: to complain to).

---

* So for a good prank, hide a pro's shoes.

Soigneurs are in charge of room keys, so they do their best at matchmaking. If there's a teammate that I get along with, I might ask to room with him. But more often, if I have a roommate request, it's that I *not* be put with someone—because I've roomed with that guy before, and there was a *problem*.

Examples of roommate issues at bike races over the years (I'm naming names!):

Disagreements over bedtime: I've had roommates who turn out the lights at 8 p.m., and then I'm sneaking around trying not to wake them. Others stay up until midnight and set their alarm for 11 minutes before we have to leave for the race, so they're getting dressed, pouring cereal down their throats, and barely making it to the bus, Will Routley.

TV: There are humans who just like to have the TV on—for noise or company—even if they're not paying attention to it, such as my grandma and Jake Rytlewski.

FaceTime: I respect a family man, until Tom Danielson is doing an hour with his kids while I'm trying to read.

Snoring: Deal breaker, Tom Zirbel.

Temperature disputes: There's a Euro myth that air conditioning is bad for your health. (Circulating air between hotel rooms can spread disease!) I love you, André Cardoso, but at the Tour de San Luis, when it's 110 degrees, we need a little breeze.

Disputes are easily settled, though. Until you find a more compatible partner, whoever's higher in the team pecking order gets final say. Cardoso was lucky he was ninth overall at San Luis, or I'd have blasted that AC and we'd both have Ebola.

Q What might make a rider unpopular in the peloton, aside from the obvious things we can see on TV?

You probably know about the hierarchy in the peloton that determines which team gets to ride where. But there is also a subtler version that might be hard to see. For example, sprinters should get the hell out of the way as we approach a mountaintop finish, you won't see me elbowing Greipel for position in the last 2 kilometers, and a certain American is soon to be hated by a handful of former teammates for telling *VeloNews* readers that they snore.

Q What are your favorite pre-race and post-race meals?

Most races provide the basic stuff like pastas and oatmeal. It's always funny to eat at a race buffet, where they serve pretty much what any lazy, single, 30-year-old male (me) would cook for himself every day, and look over to see Cavendish or Sagan eating the same crap, as if they're not millionaires who could do better. I'd order room service every night if I had their contracts. In fact, that would be in my contract.

But there's an important component that you left out: Who's paying for this hypothetical meal?

If I'm paying, Thai is the night-before dinner of choice: plenty of carbs, gluten-free options, and always delicious (I've racked up at least 10 wins on yellow curry). For breakfast, it's hard to beat Waffle House, and after the race, there's something about Mexican food. Well, it's the salt and the lard, of course, but no cheese, because my nutritionist says I'm off lactose.

If someone else is paying, you can go much classier. I love sushi the night before a race, but filling up on sushi is hard on the wallet. For breakfast and post-race—well, now that I think about it, no matter who's paying I'd still want Waffle House and Mexican food, but just to make it more expensive, I'd get extra grits and a top-shelf margarita. And I'd tip big.

Q What's been the biggest adjustment in returning to the WorldTour?

The descents can be pretty serious in Europe. In the U.S., there's not much of a pecking order, and races are less organized, so guys who just upgraded to Cat. II will come underneath you in a corner and might end up literally underneath you if they screw up. In Europe, teams ride together, so they're single file, and the guy on the front usually knows the descent. You can trust them, but it takes a few races to get used to. My first descent in Europe was at a rainy one in Mallorca. I made it in the front split, but my knuckles were white at the bottom.

Q Every time I ride, I finish with grease on my leg. How do you spend all that time on a bike but never have a chain touch your calves?

It probably helps to be a climber like me and have skinny legs. My teammate Joe Dombrowski has never had grease on his because he doesn't have calf muscles, but guys like André Greipel and Jeremy Powers have their work cut out for them.

One trick is not to worry about your legs touching your chain but rather to focus on keeping the chain clean. Our team mechanics wash the bikes daily so we don't get that grimy buildup.

When I get home, it's not that easy. Busting out the soap and bucket for the bike is a mighty struggle, so bike grease is a disease that spreads like herpes at my house (once, at a race after-party, I rode a stranger's bike and caught both). The only way to completely avoid grease stains would be to dress in all black.

Q We hear a lot about motorcycles hitting riders in races, but how do team cars pass the field to get up to the breakaway on such narrow roads? Isn't that dangerous?

You know when you're driving a car on a congested road and a police siren goes on behind you, so everyone politely pulls over in the shoulder to let it pass? Well for team cars trying to get around the pack, it's the exact opposite of that.

When the breakaway's gap reaches a minute, the commissaire tells the directors that they're allowed to go up, and each director takes a deep breath. The guy driving the car is the same one who told his rider to get in the break, but he secretly regrets it now.

The director picks a side, drives up close to the group, and starts honking. The early break has just gone, so riders all know it's the least important time to have good position, but it's still hard to make anyone budge. If he gets lucky, the road will get wider or the field will speed up and go single file. When he sees daylight, he floors it, but usually the car moves up an inch at a time (or in Europe, 2.54 cm at a time), and he lets loose with the horn while riders shout at each other to make room.

You might have noticed that many team cars have those loud, novelty custom horns, like the French equivalent of the "Dukes of Hazzard." Do you think that's meant as entertainment for the fans? I'm pretty sure it's to be as annoying as possible, because that's their only hope of getting riders to let them through.

Unlike the motorcycle drivers who seem to be bent on murder, it's not too scary when team cars come up, because WorldTour directors are all former pros with years of experience surfing a pack. The only harm is that they're often forced to pass with two wheels in the ditch on the side of the road, which sprays riders with dirt or gravel. But we deserve it, because we should have gone in the break.

Q **When you're carbo-loading before a big training ride, fuck,* marry, kill: pancake, waffles, toast.**

Kill pancakes. Pancakes are the frozen yogurt of breakfasts: only good for what you put on them. Fuck waffles. Waffles are a special-occasion breakfast dish, and they're often the saving grace of a cheap hotel in America, but you don't want them every day. Marry toast. Toast is there for you. It's simple,

---

* In the magazine, it said "f***" and people were very confused.

easy, and reliable. You can trust toast. The only exception is in Belgium, where they fuck waffles, marry waffles, and kill waffles. They've never heard of pancakes, toast, or meat.

Q What do you talk about in the breakaway, and how do you have the energy to talk when you are going that hard?

Once the breakaway is established, the pack doesn't want to catch it until the very end, so they'll keep the gap at between 2 and 10 minutes, depending on the size of the breakaway and the length of the course. The guys on the front of the pack hear the time splits, so if the breakaway slows, they'll slow down as well. You'd have trouble getting caught if you wanted to.

So getting into the breakaway can be a bitch, but you'd be surprised how easy it gets once you settle in. With a big gap and hours to go, you don't quite chat about your family or trade cookie recipes like you might in the peloton, but you can talk about the course, tactics, teammates, perhaps even negotiate trades for energy bars.

In the breakaway, each rider has his own race to deal with. You have to pace yourself to finish and save energy to win in case it sticks (it won't, but we have to pretend!).

Arguments do come up when someone isn't doing his share of the work, and with tired dudes, it can escalate. I once told a guy that if he was any good, he'd be at the Giro instead of in the breakaway at nationals. We had 40 miles to go, and it was awkward after that.

Q Do you eat all of the cookies that fans bring you at races? Are you afraid that you'll test positive after eating them?

First of all, if I ate all the cookies, my power-to-weight ratio would plummet, and I'd quickly lose my job. Second, I don't see anyone going through the trouble of tainting my baked goods so I test positive. What's the motive for that crime, exactly? I'm more afraid of taking a snack from a deranged cycling fan and then waking up tied to a chair in his basement. So no, I don't eat treats from complete strangers.*

Q During stage races, some riders take the time trial as an opportunity to save their legs. Who's in charge of deciding if you go hard or easy? Does it bother you when you're not allowed to race?

---

* I had to lie here so my team wouldn't get mad. I don't think I ever got a cookie from a stranger and didn't at least taste it, unless it had butterscotch or cranberries or something.

In the WorldTour, I'd estimate that only a quarter of the riders are really going for their best result in the time trials. We all know who the favorites are, and in races that come down to one percent and marginal gains, when the peloton doesn't have magic recovery juice like it used to, we try to save our legs as often as possible.

Team directors give every rider a job on every stage, from covering breakaways to supporting climbers to leading out sprinters to asking Twitter followers to bring cookies for mechanics and soigneurs. These jobs take energy, so if you're not high in the GC and you're not likely to crack the top 20 in the stage, you're more than happy to ride slower in the time trial and save your energy for a day that might be more fruitful. In fact, if they told me to go suffer and hurt myself when there was nothing to gain, that would be more of a bother.

The only downside is remembering the hours I spent in a wind tunnel perfecting my position, the yoga sessions to increase flexibility in my shoulders and thereby decrease my frontal area, and the research that Cannondale, Mavic, and Castelli put into the aerodynamics of the gear we ride. All of the money and man-hours there culminates with me riding at 80 percent, waving to my friends at the turnaround.

Wait, that's not a downside. That's hilarious.

Q I've seen riders who appear overweight being ridiculed in the media. You've said that you were obese before you started riding. Do you think that fat shaming is a problem in cycling?

On one hand, it's obviously not nice to tease someone for being fat, but power-to-weight is literally our job, so it's understandable when the media reports on it. Readers should separate what's expected from pro cyclists—who are monitored by doctors and nutritionists—with the bodies of the general public or average racer, who don't have any reason to be that lean.

If you're actually overweight and you want to be faster, don't starve yourself into a disorder. Instead, eat right, exercise, take your time, and get healthy.

Maybe it's not right for everyone, but I'd like to thank the people who shamed me in high school when I was obese. It pushed me to make better decisions, and for all I know, it saved my life.

Q Why do so many WorldTour riders live in Girona? Do all of you learn the native language of Catalan?

Legend has is that Lance Armstrong and his fellow pilgrims originally settled Girona, seeking refuge from their homeland, where they had been persecuted for their belief that doping was okay. The natives welcomed them with open arms and shared their bountiful harvest, but when the EPO era ended, riders stayed for the plentiful coffee shops, empty roads, and cheap apartments.

Nowadays, there are many English-speaking pros in this city. If my training calls for a three-hour ride with two hard climbs, I'll shoot out a group text and inevitably someone will want to join me (more often, when I want gelato, a partner in crime is only 500 meters away).

The Cannondale-Drapac service course is conveniently located just outside of town, and mechanics are always on hand to wash my bike or change a flat, so it's hard to imagine living anywhere else (they would kill me if I showed up at the service course asking them to change a flat).

I've picked up some Catalan, but I was sad to learn that my two semesters of Spanish were more useful at home in Los Angeles than in Girona. Here, they're almost offended when you speak Spanish—like how a New York accent might get you a dirty look in Alabama. A few guys have taken Catalan classes to properly assimilate. When I went out to eat with Trek-Segafredo's Peter Stetina, he ordered off the Catalan menu, but I consider that showing off.

I do think we should have a holiday on the fourth Thursday every July, when the pilgrims sit down and break bread with the natives to celebrate the blessings of our life in the New World. We'd eat Iberian ham instead of turkey.

Q What's the worst meal you ever had at a race? What about the best?

The worst race meal I've had was at the Tour of Trinidad, where the buffet one night consisted of baked beans and white bread. I convinced a few Americans to accompany me on a restaurant search into Port of Spain, and when word got out, a peloton of twenty guys on carbon bikes zoomed into town in the dark. We landed at a T.G.I. Friday's, where I ate a bacon burger and fries. On the way back, we passed a park where food trucks offered pizza, cotton candy, and ice cream. So it was the same night, but that was the best meal I've ever had at a race.

Q My son wants some wheels for his road bike as a gift. He likes Mavic, and since they're your team's sponsor, I figure you've tried them all and could recommend a model. Or should I just give him some money to pick them out himself?

WorldTour lunch stop.

Whatever you do, don't ask your son this question. He'll pocket the cash, buy the cheapest wheels, and spend the rest on porn or fireworks or some other contraband. Instead, buy him a set of the Cosmic Pro Carbons. The wheels are fast, they look cool, and they won't break the bank. Parents shouldn't go into debt buying bike gear for their kids, and you want the clinchers, because you don't want to pick him up on the side of the road when he has a flat. If he pocketed your cash, he may end up at a strip club or in a gutter after an overdose. See, I just saved a family.

Q You've been posting on social media about disc brakes this year. What's the verdict? Better? Worth all the drama? Do you want to race on them?

I didn't want to answer this before because it's touchy, but someone's asked me every month, so here goes.

I spent most of the year living in an apartment at the top of the hill by the cathedral in Girona, where the streets are all cobblestones and a truck comes every morning to pour water on them. I don't know what that achieves, or how Spain can meticulously water the cobbles but can't muster the energy to keep the supermarket open for an

I did hard workouts on my bike in Girona, but nothing compared to carrying groceries up these stairs.

extra 90 seconds to ring up my groceries when siesta just started.*

Sorry, I'm hungry and that got cathartic, but every morning my ride started with a 5-minute descent on slippery, wet cobblestones, through narrow roads, full of tourists looking up at their selfie sticks instead of where they're going (more catharsis). In the spring, I'd grab my rear brake, unclip one foot, and slide around the turns just to freak them out. When Cannondale sent me the disc bike, I didn't think I'd notice a difference, but it took the corners with ease, I could barely get the thing to skid, and tourists didn't even flinch when I came down the hill.

So I did my training on the disc bike, and I promise that they're better for 99.99 percent of my readers here. The 0.01 is because I had dinner with Kiel Reijnen last night, and he mentioned that he reads this (hi, Kiel!). Kiel is part of a small minority of cyclists who race in a pack of dudes who sometimes crash and pile into each other, and riders are hesitant to add sharp objects to this mix.

---

* Seriously, the grocery store is locked up at noon. There's no getting used to it.

I personally think that improved braking will reduce the number of these pileups, which will outweigh the risk of disc brakes as a whole, especially as technology improves. As more pros give discs a shot, they'll come to agree, but until then, I'll keep training on them and the tourists will thank me.

Q Do you think Grand Tour stages should be shorter?

Since I've started paying attention, Grand Tours have been won by big margins. There's one guy who's the best climber, and he just keeps putting more time on everyone until they give up and explain that they're sick (because you need an excuse to be second-best at the toughest event in the world).* If organizers wanted to add suspense or excitement in the GC, they would shorten the courses until the margin of victory is small enough that every stage matters.

Shorter stages appeal to me as a guy who does bike races, because sometimes it gets to be a bit much, but I have

---

* Quintana said he was sick at the 2016 Tour de France, and Contador was getting medical tests to find out what was wrong because he wasn't leading the Giro after two weeks. If you're in the top 10 at a Grand Tour, I'm pretty sure you're at the peak of health. Knock it off with the weird excuses.

to admit that there's something sacred about ridiculously epic stages, which Grand Tours have to balance against the suspense factor. Maybe more people would tune in next year if Froome was sprinting Quintana for intermediate time bonuses, but in the long run, if the Tour de France wasn't way too long—if it wasn't locked in a battle with the Giro and the Vuelta for who can find the steepest, silliest mountaintop finishes—it would probably lose its overall charm.

Q How do teams do selections for Grand Tours? Is it as competitive as it looks? Are there a lot of hurt feelings? Do you want to do the Tour de France someday?

Grand Tour selection is much like an elimination reality TV show. It starts early, with a "long list" of riders who are instructed to train and prepare as if they're guaranteed a spot (which means some guys will train for months, only to miss it). And when I say the long list is determined early, I think Vaughters wrote the one for 2014 sometime during the Reagan administration.

The list is then slowly thinned out based on how guys are riding, performance at training camps, power testing, health, how they get along with the group, and probably a million other factors that I can't imagine. Occasionally, a rider who missed the long list wins something and horses his way into the Tour, but it's rare. At the end, the team sport directors look at race results and power data, and do an analysis to take the best squad they can, so it can be second-guessed on social media by people who don't know anything.

Of course I want to do the Tour de France, or any Grand Tour. I was on the list for the Vuelta this year, along with 14 other guys. In June, I fasted for a week to increase my fat-burning efficiency.* In July, I trained my ass off, including a 3-week solo altitude camp, which included lots of intervals and heat-specific training, frying myself on the road every day because Spain is scorching in August and I wanted to be acclimated. My legs were good. And then one day, they told me I was off the list.

I was bummed, but 14 other guys were putting themselves through the same kind of training, and this was what we all signed up for as pro cyclists, so I can't say I was insulted or hurt.†

And here's the other thing: While those guys were suffering through the Vuelta, I went for long rides around

---

* This is supposed to be a big predictor of success at stage races.

† I was both of those, but I tried to fake it here.

Catalunya, stopping for a sandwich at the coast, drinking coffee on the Ramblas. I'll admit that I didn't get into pro cycling for coffee. I got into it for glory and competition and adventure. But coffee is nice, too.*

---

* I had an amazing three weeks of bike tourism in Girona. Lots of crepes on the Mediterranean.

HOW TO WIN THE RACE BUFFET

1. *Coffee.* (Unless this happened in your hotel room already.)

2. *Put toast in the toaster.* That way it toasts while you're walking the buffet, and you don't have to stand there making small talk with other guys who planned their buffet poorly.

3. *Put two packets of butter in your pocket.* It's always frozen or refrigerated. If you pocket it, it'll be nice and soft when you get to your table.

4. *Grab a piece of cheese.* This is your "walking around cheese." You want something to nibble on while you explore. This helps you make good decisions, for the same reason you don't go to the grocery store hungry.

5. *Hit the buffet.* For breakfast, I go oatmeal, bacon, eggs, maybe French toast with peanut butter.

6. *Don't get any damn rice or pasta.* It's always there, but this is breakfast.

7. *But never take an eye off your toast.* It will get stolen if it pops up unclaimed. Bunch of animals at these buffets.

8. *Think about what you might want for later.* If there's a croissant or some kind of brownie thing, you'll feel like a genius if you wrap it in a napkin and pull it out 100km into the stage.

9. *Pick up your toast.* Or steal someone else's. Whatever. We're animals.

10. *Don't forget silverware.* I've had many a long walk from the table back to the buffet because I didn't notice the silverware/napkin roll.

APPENDIX B

A GUIDE TO HOST HOUSING

Race organizers often arrange host housing for riders as a way to manage the costs for small teams. These wonderful folks got me through a few rough years, and once I started writing about it, some families said that they were thinking of volunteering their home for a team, and they wanted to know what exactly would be expected of them.

What cyclists would want from a host family.

A bed: It can be an air mattress, but I want sheets and a pillow. You can't do a stage race in sleeping bags, unless you're me in 2008, but that was ugly. Don't make the bed. Just put the sheets on top and I'll take care of it. Just act like your weirdo cousin is coming to stay. He doesn't get royal treatment because you don't want him to stay too long, but he gets the basics.

A towel: Towels are good.

Fridge and counter space: Just go through and throw out all the expired salad dressings, and there'll be enough room for my almond milk and eggs. A foot or so of counter space will do it.

Space: No more than two (maaaaybe three) to a room. I think a lot of race promoters just ask a family how many square feet they have, and see it as a challenge to Tetris as many air mattresses in a room as they can (or they pressure them to hold more than they should). It's okay for a night or two, but if it's a long trip, we need to not feel like we're sitting on a Southwest flight for a week. The best situation has been when one family agrees to host and then asks their neighbors if they can each house a couple more. That way, we have one house that's a base for cooking, massage, and mechanics, but we get to spread out on the block.

Washer/dryer access: We have some stinky stuff.

Trust: I've heard of hosts who don't let the riders into their house if they're not home, so guys are sitting on the porch calling them when the race is over. We're not going to steal anything. Maybe I'll grab a cookie if you leave it on the counter, but that's entrapment.

Wi-Fi: Otherwise, what are we supposed to do at dinner? Talk to each other?

What host families should avoid.
Spending money: If you want to cook every meal for us, you're a saint, but it's by no means expected. I've had hosts constantly apologizing for not doing enough, and I think a lot of people hesitate to take on a team because they think it'll be costly. But it shouldn't cost you a dime, and you really don't have to burn a calorie.

Noise: Don't host if you have a crying baby, crazy barking dogs, or a 16-year-old learning the drums.

Filth: I don't need to eat off the floor, and clutter is fine, but I don't want to be covered in cat hair, either. I've had a couple stage races ruined by allergies, probably from sleeping on air mattresses in dusty rooms.

Advice for riders who stay at host housing.

Remember their names: Write it down if you have to.

Leave the house cleaner than you found it: Empty the dishwasher, even if it's not yours.

Be subtle, but let them know what a good guest you are: When you empty the dishwasher, put a few things away in the wrong place. That way, they'll know it was you that did it, and not the lazy 13-year-old daughter.

Leave a gift: That hotel would have cost you $80 a night, and a decent bottle of Cabernet is $14.

RACE WARM-UP ROUTINE

Lots of people asked me how to warm up for a race over the years. It would have been a boring question for the magazine, but here's my routine for time trials or short road races. If it's over two hours, warm-ups are for amateurs.

- Have a coffee or something with caffeine 60 minutes before the start time.

- About 40 to 45 minutes before your start, start riding easy, ideally on a trainer, just turning the legs.

- When you're loose, pedal harder until your heart rate reaches 120.

- The second you see 120 on the heartrate monitor, shut it off and turn the legs again real easy.

- When you're fresh again (this won't take more than a couple minutes that early in the routine), pedal harder until your heart rate touches 130, then again totally shut it down and pedal easy.

- Keep upping the effort every time you're fresh, by 10-beat increments.

- When you get within 15 beats of the HR you time trial at (or if it's taking a little longer than you want to respond), start going by 5-minute increments.

- Once you've touched or passed your TT heart rate, shut it down again, spin the legs until they're fresh, and head to the start.

TOO HOT FOR *VELONEWS*

I sent this in for the magazine column one month, but Neal Rogers, the editor at the time, thought it was distasteful. After all the poop and pee and fart jokes, here's where he finally drew the line and refused to publish something. I put it in every column I submitted for the next year, just to screw with him, but Neal was vigilant.

Q **You don't have firsthand knowledge of this, but I thought you might know anyway. I've seen men pee off the bike during races with a push from their teammates, but what do women do when they have to go during a race?**

Indeed, as a male, this question is foreign to me, but I asked around for a good answer. From what I've gathered, [deleted by VeloPress].

ACKNOWLEDGMENTS

I'd like to thank Neal Rogers, John Bradley, and Chris Case at *VeloNews*, and Ted Costantino at VeloPress, as well as all the other editors, proofreaders, and interns who worked with my copy over the years.

To my readers: This column was my first paid writing gig, and I hope you enjoyed it as much as I did. Most importantly, now that you have all the answers, go ride a bike. Remember, it's not what you know. It's what you do.

THE PHIL COOKIE

12 cookies, 180 grams each / *Created by chef Jeff Mahin, this recipe combines peanut butter, chocolate chips, and pretzels into a Phil-approved Pro Cookie. Jeff is the creator of Stella Barra Pizzeria and Do-Rite Donuts, a regular guest on the Food Network's "Sugar Showdown," and an ambassador for Chefs Cycle.*

COOKIE DOUGH

⅔ pound unsalted butter, room temperature (275 grams)
1⅓ cup granulated sugar (255 grams)
1 cup dark brown sugar (255 grams)
18 ounces smooth peanut butter (510 grams)
2 eggs, room temperature
1 vanilla bean, scraped
2 cups all-purpose flour (250 grams)
1¾ teaspoon sea salt (9 grams)
1½ teaspoon baking powder (6 grams)
½ tablespoon baking soda (6 grams)
8–9 ounces 72-percent chocolate, in pistoles or chips (250 grams)
1 cup dry-roasted peanuts, chopped (150 grams)

1. Place the butter and sugars into a mixer fitted with a paddle attachment and mix at medium speed until light and fluffy.
2. Add peanut butter and continue to mix.
3. Lower the mixer speed and add eggs and scrapings from the vanilla bean.
4. Combine all dry ingredients and sift to make sure there are no clumps.
5. Add dry ingredients to the mixer and mix until combined; do not over-mix.
6. Add chocolate and peanuts; mix until combined.

FLOUR